HOME OF KNEW-AGE POETRY

THE
POETRY
SHACK

JAMES L. THOMPSON, JR.

Book cover designed by GetCovers.com

Front cover custom painting by Justin Lockley (jlockley@live.com)

ISBN: 979-8-9877718-4-6 – paperback

Printed in the United States

www.peanutcitypress.com

Philadelphia, PA and Dothan, AL

PEANUT CITY PRESS
TELLING OUR STORIES ®

This book is dedicated to all past, present, and future poets. Always remember that: *"The wings of a butterfly are merely the dreams-come-true of an optimistic caterpillar."* JLT, Jr.

CONTENTS

PREFACE

This deluxe all-poetry book is a first for me in many years. While poetry is my first love, I know that may not be true for the average reader. As a poet, I try not to write complicated poems with wild, abstract verses. I believe that poetry is like little slices of life with or without whipped cream. In this new expanded volume, you will find a mixture of these slices of life that touch on: serious, funny, sad, political, historical, satirical, religious, love, hate, and knew. There's something for everyone here and I hope you take the time to share what you read with others. Thank you for investing your hard-earned time and money into purchasing The Poetry Shack. Hopefully, you will not regret it.

Yours truly,
James L. "Shack" Thompson, Jr.

"THE POETRY SHACK"

Welcome to the Poetry Shack,
The home of Knew-Age poetry.
Coffee and poems are the perfect snack
But if you prefer, we also have tea.

Always open with a fresh morning brew,
Poetry and coffee provide a new outlook
And help you to discover the real you
Within the pages of a realistic book.

Coffee beans or tea bags are your choice
To help you swallow the rhymes and the reasons.
You may also discover your hidden voice
In our poetry for all times and all seasons.

There's nothing better than a hot cup of Joe
With a good book of poetry.
They pick us up when we are low
And help to restore our symmetry.

The smell from the coffee tempts our palette
And helps to refine our taste.
The words from the book prove to be valid
When we think of all the memories we face.

Effective poetry tends to transform us
And our fantasies come into view
Anything we can imagine is a plus
To proclaim the poet's verses are true.

The rhythm and cadence of each verse
Make our heart beat with every sip.
The lines of the poet are meant to coerce
And the coffee entices with the very first drip.

So, start your day with a dynamic pair
Coffee and poetry are a perfect match.
Have more than one cup if you dare
And remember to savor each and every batch.

"A Knew Poem"

There's nothing really new about this poem

Except that it is being read by you for the first time.

I wrote it yesterday for the first time,

But I didn't know if it would be good enough for you.

So, I threw in a couple of "knew" words like,

"I Luv you" and "Furever"

But you already knew that, didn't you?

"WRITE LIKE SMOKEY"

Oh, if I could write like Smokey or sing like Marvin, I'd be okay

Bob Dylan said Smokey was *America's greatest living poet*

Most would agree but then Dylan had never met Marvin Gaye

Smokey has a special way with his lyrics and can smoothly show it

Neither Marvin nor Smokey were known for their dancing

They were both balladeers whose voices spun solid gold

All their slow songs were tailor-made for romancing

Between the two of them millions of hit records were sold

Both were known for their silky singing and their sex appeal

They were Motown's lethal weapons when it came to hits

For label mates, The Originals, Marvin wrote *Baby I'm For Real*

Later lead singer Smokey left The Miracles and called it quits

What's Going On and *Quiet Storm* are two of my favorite picks

Both songs transcend time and are relevant to this very day

The lyrics to both songs and the music are what really sticks

Others may listen to new music but it's the old songs I like to play

I guess there's no doubt who my two favorite Motown singers are
There are far too many to choose from but these two resonate with me
Singers come and singers go and some even earn the title of star
But Smokey and Marvin are first name icons and with Stevie they make three

"PLEA BARGAIN"

Sitting down looking up at the blue-gray sky

Wondering if you're ever going to forgive me—

God knows I can't think of a good reason why

But hoping one day we can agree to disagree;

The rusty old swing set sways in the wind

As the weeds snake their way around its feet—

A year's gone by since you were my friend

I long for the days when things were sweet;

Whatever tore us apart I hope can be repaired

I miss your smile, your laugh and your disposition—

Give me another chance for my love to be declared

And make a lasting change in our current condition;

A beggar's plea is based on art instead of science

My heart is the thermostat for my emotions—

I'm betting we can make a beautiful alliance

One rooted in love, faith and everlasting devotion;

Mistakes are bound to be made in any affair

Forgiveness is the key to a brand-new start—

Please accept my plea if you dare

And I'll love you forever with all my heart.

"BENCH WARRANT"

T
H
E

P
O
E
T
R
Y

S
H
A
C
K

14

My wife is a judge in Superior Court
I am a pilot for the airline industry
When making love, we usually abort
Our plans for starting a big family

She works days and I work nights
Like two ships, we often pass each other by
Our time apart has caused many fights
Desperate, my wife found something new to try

My wife issued a bench warrant for my arrest
In order to make me comply to her demand
She didn't have too much time to invest
To try and finally make me understand

With cuffed hands and an ankle bracelet on
I was refused my right to arrange for any bail
I was not even allowed to use our home telephone
She wanted to make it clear that I was in jail

Finally, at night we spent some time alone
Intimate and satisfying, our love was in flight
She judged me as I piloted her erogenous zone
After one night together, we never had another fight

Legally, the court said she overstepped her bounds
And entrapped me to make me do her will
I objected and innocent she was found
For another bench warrant, I am guilty still

"Flying Above Adversity"
(Tribute to the Tuskegee Airmen)

Like Buffalo Soldiers in the sky,
the Tuskegee Airmen flew very high;

High above all the adversity
and on toward making history;

Black men trained at segregated facilities,
only served to increase their abilities;

On freedom's wings bound for glory,
they created their own incredible story;

They excelled in the Tuskegee Experiment
to show their bravery was no accident;

Their heroism on and off the battlefield
proved vital in leveling the playing field;

Their place now secured in American history,
no longer regarded as a military mystery;

The armed services soon became integrated,
their hard-found victory now illuminated;

As the Tuskegee Airmen soared with gravity,
high above all the adversity;

A great place that they did earn,
and a great lesson for a nation to learn.

"FOREVER RUNNING FREE"

When young hearts run free
Sometimes they find something new
Like the discovery of you and me
And the reality of deciding what to do;

The experience of looking beneath the skin
Is something we never faced until we did.
The joy of understanding that we both could win
Once we felt that the truth no longer needed to be hid;

Reaching across the aisle is apt for politicians,
But hearts are not easily legislated.
We both understood the risks and propositions,
And yet our feelings and lives were still elevated;

For a moment in time we threw the dice,
And felt our natural souls unite.
We will always remember that it was so nice
When fear was replaced with the brave moonlight;

That light still flickers and shines in our hearts and minds
Like a flame that will last forever.
We feel the love as the clock rewinds
And reminds us that our love is maturer;

If young hearts are allowed to run free
Then mature ones should be allowed to surrender.
Yesterday it was all about you and me
And today, after all this time, our hearts still remember.

"Love Songs' Desperate Plagiarism"

My eyes can clearly see
You no longer care for me
The closer I get to you
Neither one of us know what to do
But you're the first to say goodbye

Betcha by golly wow
If I only knew how
To get you back in my life
And restore my happy wife
With ribbons in the sky

Ooh baby, baby
What does it take to win your love
Let's stay together
You're all I need to get by
We've come too far to end it now

We've gone through the agony
And I'm now waiting for the ecstasy
If you don't know me by now
I need your precious love
And all your fire and desire

Our love is like a quiet storm

I'm caught up in all your charm

Oh girl, I'm so proud of you

What becomes of the broken hearted

La-La means I love you

It's an optical conclusion

I'm in a ball of confusion

Love is such a heavy load

This is our fork in the road

It's a thin line between love and hate

"MALCOLM EX"

Her first husband was named Malcolm;

all her friends nicknamed him Malcolm Ex

He had a smooth voice like Dr. King,

but he cheated on her and his wedding ring

He often scored by any means necessary,

and his favorite position was the Missionary.

Malcolm was gunned down by a jealous lover,

he was caught red-handed while under cover.

His death was not mourned by the whole Nation

due to his predilection for shameless flirtation.

She decided never to marry again,

saying she couldn't be sure where the next man had been

The moral of this story is not so perplexed

because there are many guys out there like Malcolm Ex.

"Epitaphs"

From Strange Fruit hanging from poplar trees
To Black men dying on their "I Can't Breathe" knees,
Black men are still considered an endangered species —
While crying out for their Mommas.

Life for them ain't been no crystal stair or diamond ring,
Ahmaud Arbery, George Floyd, Tyre Nichols and Rodney King
Modern day Black men beaten on camera —
While heard crying out for their Mommas.

For the Emmett Tills, our tears are full
But our emotional cupboards are bare;
Because we know —
There is no justice for them anywhere.

We currently live in a futuristic past where horrific events
Are on par with current events in this 21st century.
Black lives matter… White lives matter… Blue lives matter…
All lives matter… is just idle chatter;
Because at the end of this non-stop trajectory —
No lives really matter.

"I'm Not George Floyd"

At the local grocery,
I watched a man being demanded to
raise his hands in the air as he
loudly declared, "I'm not George Floyd...
I'm not George Floyd. Damn!"
He was being profiled because
he had a suspicious-looking face
that didn't fit, and the money he was
carrying looked suspiciously like counterfeit.

At my neighborhood bank,
I saw another man under arrest
for trying to cash a skeptical-looking
$500 check that he claimed was his paycheck.
He too raised his hands on demand and declared,
"I'm not George Floyd... I'm not George Floyd. Damn!"

Shopping at the mall,
I bought an expensive pair of shoes
with my credit card and was immediately
suspected of having stolen it.
Security guards ordered me to put
my hands behind my back as
I heard myself loudly declare,
"I'm not George Floyd... I'm not George Floyd. Damn!"

Do we all look like George Floyd

or is that just a scapegoat?

Innocently taken away with my hands

cuffed behind my back, I again declared,

"I'm not George Floyd… I'm not George Floyd. Damn!

(But then again, I feel like I am)

"I GOT S.O.M.E."

They overpowered my ego when her shotgun-toting parents
frogmarched me down the aisle to marry her
in the peopleless church.

I looked up at the thin-collared preacher man
waiting there with Bible in hand and weaponized holy water
if I misbehaved or needed further convincing.

I arose sober and took my place standing next to her.
She wore a white dress with a black lace veil
that covered her face; I was not sure at all
who I was being forced to marry.

I remembered dancing with a girl at the party
and having a few drinks before I blacked out.
The preacher never asked me to say *I Do*
and must have assumed that I already did.

Her parents slid the rings on our fingers and
forbade me to kiss the bride, saying that too much
kissing was the reason I was there in the first place.

The next thing I knew we were married and on our
way to the moon without any honey.

By the way, I later learned that I was part of a
SIZE OBVIOUSLY MATTERS EXPERIMENT since I
was six-feet-two and she was only four-feet-ten.
And we lived happily ever after her parents untied me.

"WALKING HOME FROM SCHOOL"

In 8th grade, I walked slowly behind her every day after school

Although we walked the same way, I kept my distance and my cool

I hadn't learned how to say I like you and I didn't have any swag

Instead of a backpack, I carried my books in a brown paper bag

I could tell she liked me too and was waiting for me to make a move

My tongue was tied, my lips chapped, and I was not very smooth

Once she stopped to tie her shoe to give me a sign

I kept walking like I didn't see and acted like I was blind

In 9th grade, I decided to clear my throat

She smiled at me and then slipped me a note

Her note asked me if I could walk her home the next day

I smiled and replied, "Yeah, since we're going the same way."

From that day forward, we began to court

And I became her one and only escort

We walked together all year long in any kind of weather

If offered a ride, we'd both shake our heads and say never

For walking home from school was our special time together

We walked on clouds and stepped as light as a feather

At the end of the road, we shared our first sweet kiss

That was a long time ago, but yet I still vividly reminisce

"The Kool Kids"

They were so cool that they spelled the word cool with a K

They never studied or did homework for being busy at play

Both boys and girls just trying to be hip

Until they decided to take another kind of trip

First it started with a tobacco cigarette

And later on, they decided to increase the bet

Illegal cigarettes among them started to flow

And the next thing that came was something called blow

They were the coolest kids in all the schools

Who became known as the stupidest fools

When it came to tests, they usually failed

The next thing you know they all got expelled

Standing on the outside now looking in

They were no longer Kool and they couldn't pretend

The lesson to be learned here to this very day

Is that the word cool begins with a C and not with a K

"The Clock of the Bay"

Sitting on a clock at the bay
Killing time but doing it my way
Being careful not to move an arm
Not yet ready to set off the alarm

I've got a time bomb under my seat
If I move, I'll probably lose my feet
Not sure how I made it to this point
I usually come here just to smoke a joint

Sea gulls laughing out on the water
They sense my fuse is getting shorter
Sharks gathering around me to stay
They are ready for their human buffet

My mind is about to be completely blown
At least I won't actually die alone
This may look and feel like suicide
Please tell my family that I really tried

My heart beats faster as time counts down
If the bomb doesn't kill me, maybe I'll drown
My life has been underwhelming at best
This final blast will lay me to rest

I wish I had selected a smarter way
Than sitting on this time clock at the bay
The time will come soon for me to go
Any second now and it's going to blow

"The Call of the Sheep"

It seems like lately many of my friends are dying
and the Good Shepherd is calling in his sheep
At night, I ask Him to protect me and my loved ones
as we close our eyes for the night's sleep
I know that our time on Earth is precious
and each of us has our day
I only pray that when my time comes,
I'm home with my family and not somewhere away

Many have died in accidents
or taken during a long illness at hand
Some even lost their lives in battle
fighting for the freedom of our land
I know our days are numbered
and no man knows when that time is set
Yet, I hope that my life on Earth
has been meaningful with not a single regret

Death is part of the big cycle of life
and no one should be dismayed
The one thing we can all hope for
is that our deaths will slowly be delayed
The call of the sheep is inevitable
so we can no longer roam
And once we all get there,
we can rejoice in our eternal home

"In Memory Of Him"

I lost my best friend a decade ago
He was the one I always confided in
It's hard to believe that it's actually so
I still hurt today like I hurt then

We attended the same college together
He was my Best Man and I was his
He was more reliable than the weather
I learned from him what friendship is

His sense of humor was infectious
He acted like my biological brother
He was brave, proud but never pretentious
Everyone knew we were meant for each other

I never thought he would leave first
And I would have to go it all alone
I don't think I could feel any worse
If I was the one who instead had gone

I'm praying that we will meet again
And resume where life separated us
I never intend to find a better friend
We knew each other for fifty years plus

In memory of Him whom I loved so much
What I would give to laugh with him again
He had a big voice but a gentle touch
I was blessed the day he became my friend

"NOSTALGIA"

I'm in love with amazing Nostalgia
She's so much more than a side piece
In Latin, her name is similar to Miranda
Worthy of admiration and hard to release

> Old-fashioned with a dream of yesterday
> Is my desire to live in the past
> Where life was simple and a better way
> To take it easy to make things last

Turning the clock back is no fairytale
For dreams and wishes can come true
One day soon I am going to prevail
And finally find that place called Xanadu

> I want to go back and remain there forever
> Born too soon, I'm not with this New Age
> It's all brand-new and high-tech clever
> But it still feels like a modern-day cage

I live for Mission Impossible and The Twilight Zone
Gunsmoke, Rawhide, and Bonanza are close behind
They entertained when we had a dial telephone
And made life so effortless to unwind

> Nostalgia is holding my hand for one last ride
> I don't believe I'm ever coming back
> I've decided where I really want to reside
> With luggage in hand, I start my fade-to-black

"Sweet Lady In The Moon"

I gazed at the moon because I was in love

I saw something there that I never dreamed of

The man in the moon was not standing alone

The lady in his arms must have been his own

A lady in the moon for a celestial mate

Falling in love is never too late

Sweet lady in the moon is fit for a queen

A moonlit sky is a beautiful scene

"No Rhymes, No Reasons"

This poem does not rhyme because we no longer rhyme together;
I lost my rhythm when I unconsciously lost you.

Poetry has no meaning when the reasons for it have gone away;
I couldn't buy a rhyme if I wanted to because the loss has left me broke.

When a poet loses his rhymes, he is no longer considered a poet;
I am a man holding an empty pen with a blank piece of paper.

Everything I wrote in the past was about my loving you;
I don't know how to write about anything else since my reasons have left.

Without any real purpose, I voluntarily surrender to Writer's Block;
I will never write another word until you come back or until I perish.

Please, I respectfully request no words to be written on my tombstone;
I became a blank slate in life when you left me alone with nothing.

Blaming you for the way my life is ending is probably unfair;
I must also accept the fault of letting the flame grow cold.

It's so much easier to blame you for this feeling of desertion;
I stand accused of providing half the reason for your departure.

Now that you have gone, I must find another muse;
I will find that difficult since I only had one heart.

Whether you come back or not, I have learned a grave lesson;
I should let the reasons be the rhymes and not the rhymes be the reasons.

"Old Tyme Religion"

Remember when Sundays used to feel like Sundays

And there was an honest-to-goodness

Natural reverence inside churches?

We had special clothes we wore and

We didn't work or shop on the Sabbath.

Preachers tried to save as many souls

As they could without collecting

from the collection plates first.

"Give me that old time religion"

Was more than just a song.

There were worn out church hymnals,

Wicker basket collection plates,

And hard wooden pews.

Neighbors helped neighbors

When times were hard and kinfolk

Acted like blood was thicker than water.

Mega churches did not exist and

Prosperity preaching was not a *Thing*.

Blind faith was real and we believed in

A heaven and a hell like

The Good Book references.

We respected our elders and

We didn't talk ill of the dead.

There was no such thing as the *Me Generation;*

We believed that God was bigger than us

And that we must be born again

In order to see Him in heaven.

We gladly became our brother's keeper

And we felt good about it without

Expecting anything in return.

When we stopped to help someone

On the side of the road,

We were more afraid that we would

Lose our souls rather than

Our lives if we didn't help them.

Having that old time religion

Was a way of life that seems

To have died on the cross

A long time ago along with

The Golden Rule and the 10 Commandments.

"ORDAINED"

My life, created by Him
Ordained to the brim
  He salvaged my fate;
Bestowed every precious day
Allowed amazing grace to stay
And lit up my dismal way
  He is never late.

My soul lifted, free
His promise of eternity
  Heaven is waiting;
Everything I do on Earth
Beginning with my birth
Is a measure of my worth
  No more hating.

My quest for salvation
Is my life's validation
  He hears my prayers;
My heart is cleaned
From sin I am weaned
And forever quarantined
  Free from world affairs.

I pray that I am right
Pleasing unto His sight
  My heart filled with glee;
I spread the love around
Glad that I was truly found
Received my heavenly crown

"D.E.I."

Let's all get rid of DEI
and pray that it may never return
We don't need it to get by
And with it there's nothing to learn

DEI was introduced to help the rich
And push the masses further away
Entitlement programs should be ditched
Because they make us weaker in the USA

Divided we stand, together we fall
DEI is a weapon of mass destruction
It is guaranteed to destroy us all
And eliminate our intelligence production

To be clear, the D.E.I. I am referring to means:

Division. Extremism. Ignorance

Let's also destroy the FBI
And put them into the mix
The whole agency deserves to DIE
Because it investigated January six

"BLACK LACE"

He wore black lace underwear but no one ever suspected
A powerful man whose job was presidentially protected
His mission was public service and nationwide protection
He hid his secret to avoid condemnation and rejection
Cross-dressing was a double cross to his manhood and his mandate
His black lace symbolized elegance, power and his affinity to man date.

Although he wore black lace, he did not wear black face
That would have been far too much for history to erase
Secret intelligence was the primary source of his power
Many feared his wrath and, in his presence, would often cower
In all circles, he was known to be a shaker and a mover
He carved out a name for himself and was hard to outmaneuver
     In the end, his footnote in history was surreal and blighted
     Since his president was not a king, he was not likely to be knighted

"CAFFEINATED POETRY"

At the Poetry Shack,
our caffeinated poetry comes in three different blends.

Lite Roast: a blend of simple, easy, fun, and tasteful.

Medium Roast: Reflective with a little more caffeine and meat on the bones.

Heavy Roast: our strongest blend that is both thought-provoking and poignant.

Coffee and poetry both stimulate our senses with good taste,
and they often taste good while doing so.

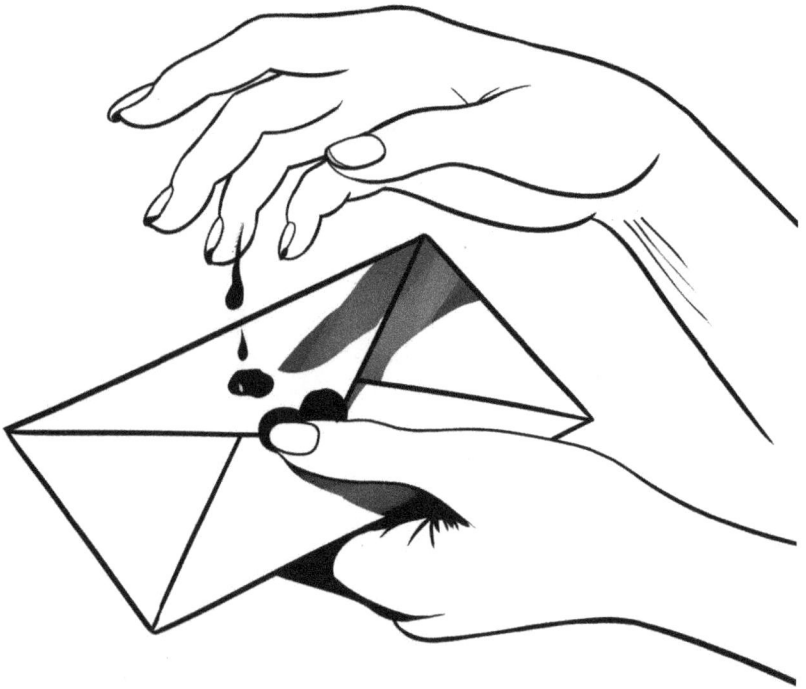

"Paper Cut From A Love Note"

She found a sealed envelope
lying on her pillow
after her lover had left her bedroom.

It still had the scent
of sex on it.

She eagerly slipped her finger
underneath the envelope
and instantly received
a painful, premonition paper cut.

Blood dripped on the page
as she opened the note to read it.

The words she read hurt more than
the cut she'd just received
on her finger.

Her lover wrote that
he was no longer in love
with her and he wasn't
coming back.

She looked at the blood
on the note which symbolized
her broken, bleeding heart.

Realizing that alcohol
would sterilize the wound
but cause further pain,
she decided to suck the blood

From her paper-cut finger
and burn the note
to cauterize the bleeding.

"MLK DAY – 1986-2025"

While he stood on Capitol Hill,
We all remained perfectly still
And listened to his dream

He envisioned a place
Unaccustomed for his Black race
One nation under God

"I've been to the mountain top"
Was the theme of his last stop
Before he fell at the Lorraine Motel

Some people called him a messiah
Others accused him of being a liar
His tainted legacy remains

His name given a national holiday
Which some now want to take away
With liberty and justice for all?

Oh, say can you clearly see
All the political hypocrisy
By the dawn's early light?

The USA has celebrated an MLK national holiday for 39 years. Ironically, both MLK and Malcolm X were 39 years old when they were assassinated.

"THE UN-TIED STATES OF AMERICA"

America is not as well-knit
When all states don't fit
     Its united claim.

Sister states sibling rivalry
Civil war over slavery
Secession by the Confederacy
     Neither side the blame

Land of the unfree
Struggling to claim liberty
     Home of the brave?

Freedom can be illusive
Justice can be delusive
Democracy can be abusive
     Flags no longer wave.

Our pledge of allegiance
Cannot withstand the malfeasance
     Throughout our model nation.

Mass shootings without gun laws
Court rulings with legal flaws
Gas lighting with political claws
     It's a critical situation.

The United States Constitution
Bears proof as the solution
     Unless it is amended.

Patriotism has been redefined

Gender roles have been reassigned

Political foes have been realigned

        The United States upended.

"Trojan Horses Are Real"

In the 12th or 13th century BC,
The Trojan War took place in the
city of Troy and left destruction
      everywhere.

When the Trojan soldiers rode in on their
Trojan horses to rape the land and its people,
they opted not to wear Trojan
      prophylactics.

In this year of our Lord,
Trojan horses are symbolically real
And they hide the enemy within
      in plain view.

From mass acceptance to mass confusion,
the people voted against their own
      independence.

Blinded by false prophecies
of making things great again
and saving our country,
we are witnessing a real live purge
of that which actually made us
      great.

By the time we realize what we all have
lost, it will be too late
to repair the damage to our lives
      and our souls.

Blame it on a mass acceptance of evil
and an acquiescence of hate
permeating our nation with
incompetence and a lack of
        morality.

How can those who are responsible
for destroying us be trusted
with rebuilding us and making us
        stronger?

There is no better parable than the fox
guarding the hen house to explain such hypocrisy.
The holy ghost is now a ghost with holes in its
soul and Little Red Riding Hood happily skips home
so her big-teeth grandma
        can devour her.

Christopher Columbus did not discover America in 1492,
but he was welcomed by some intelligent indigenous people
who had lived here for thousands of years before
        he *discovered* America.

When today's modern Trojan soldiers ride in on their
Trojan horses to rape the land and its people,
they also will opt not to wear Trojan
        prophylactics.

"WATERFALL"

With every single drop
I stop
To reflect on what you
Meant to me and how I
Wish you would've stayed.

Your calls turned into
Letters and your letters
Turned into notes,
Reminding me not to forget you
"With love."

Is there any way at all
To cushion the water's fall?

What started out as a waterfall
Turned into a Tsunami
Simply because you did not come back to me

"TSUNAMI"

40 days and 40 nights were a biblical Tsunami,
But that's also how long I cried over you;
The sponge in my heart broke apart when
It realized you were never going to be true.

> Yet, I rode the wave in order to save all the
> Self-respect and dignity that I had left;
> Rain may be good for flowers and trees,
> But too much rain from my eyes is a visual theft.

Water falling at a heavy pace can never replace
The senses with a sense of calm and belonging;
The eye of the storm and the why of the storm are like tear gas,
And the real reason the rough weather is prolonging.

> Once the rain clears and I rebound from my tears,
> I will never be caught again without my protection;
> Most often the biggest harm from a torrential storm
> Is not the loss of life but it's the loss of eventual affection.

Noah's Ark was a walk in the park for what you put me through.
For men-don't-cry is a hell-of-a-lie when you are doing the crying;
The sun is now out to stay and the clouds are moving away.
The lonely survivor weathered the storm and is intent on surviving.

> Rain is heavenly made for heavenly reasons we know,
> And humans are taught to swim and stay afloat;
> Hearts are made to live out their dreams and passions,
> But for broken hearts, there is no unsinkable antidote.

"This Is Personal"

Personally, I'm going to tell you the truth
Somehow, I let you get under my skin
This mystery doesn't require a real sleuth
You stole my heart and scored a big win

I'm not the same person I used to be
You unfroze my heart with a gentle touch
In doing so, you magically set me free
To love you always and it's never too much

Down we fall because gravity won't let us fall up,
Spiritually, we will ride across the blue sky
And eternally drink from the loving cup
I am wedded to you until the day we die

I have no one else waiting on second base
In case our love decides to take a detour
My love for you cannot be easily replaced
You are the only one and with that I am sure

I've got you and you've got me for as long as it lasts
The many years that we've spent together are our proof
I'm more concerned about our future than I am about your past
You should know by now that with you I have always told the truth

Finally, I personally have nowhere else to go if you leave
That's why this testimony is so very personal to me
There's nothing else I can say that will make you believe
My life belongs to you because you are my destiny

"PICKLE GIRL"

Angie was twelve years old and she loved to eat pickles.

She even loved drinking the pickle juice; the sourer, the better. Everyone nicknamed her *Pickle Girl* and the other children in the Bronx made fun of her because she loved pickles so much. They would often see her riding her brand-new Christmas bicycle with one hand on the handlebars while eating a pickle with the other.

In the summertime, she wore bright pastel-colored dresses and cute girly ribbons in her hair. She was not interested in boys because she thought they were dumb, especially if they did not like pickles. She believed that eating pickles was healthy and it helped with hydration by adding electrolytes; yes, she was also a super smart bookworm.

One day at the library, Angie wondered who was the largest pickle producer in the U.S. She conducted a quick search and learned that Mt. Olive Pickle Company in Mt. Olive, NC was the largest pickle producer in the U.S. with a 70% market share. She became so excited that she vowed then to move to North Carolina after college so she could work for Mt. Olive. She didn't care what position she had as long as she was located near pickles.

Angie graduated with a degree in Sales and Marketing, and immediately applied for a job at Mt. Olive. The recruiter was so impressed with her knowledge about pickles that they offered her a job as their Marketing Strategist. Within a year, Angie had devised an aggressive company marketing strategy to grow Mt. Olive's market share by another 10%. With now 80% of the country's pickle market share, Mt. Olive promoted Angie to Regional Vice President.

At North Carolina's Annual State Fair, Angie gave out free pickles to all the people and they loved her for it. Some vendors even sold fried pickles to help boost their sales. Angie spent her professional career at Mt. Olive and after 35 years, she became known as the Pickle Queen of North Carolina all over the U.S.

What a dream come true for a little girl who knew what she wanted after she took her first bite of a pickle. No one ever laughed at her or made fun of her again about her love of pickles. She did get married and had a big family with two boys and one girl. Everyone suspected that her daughter, Angelina, would also grow up to be a pickle girl just like her mother.

Angelina got a brand-new shiny bicycle for her tenth birthday with a front basket for carrying pickles and all the money she would make when she grew up to be a pickle lady.

"MISTRESS"

Poetry is my first love

and my forever mistress.

With a soft kiss,

she wakes me when

everyone else is asleep

and takes me to many beautiful,

>   secret places.

Together with love and purpose,

we procreate paper orphans to share,

but our private memories are

>   only for us to keep.

Before publication,

we carefully edit out

all the decadent parts

that we can't share

>   with the rest of the world.

"THE ERRANT SHIP"

The fool's ship runs amok
Its country's name emblazoned on its side
But what kind of ship is it?
A clipper ship from the 19th century or
A passenger ship with only the aristocracy or
A container ship without any real contents or
A battleship with an embattled crew?
Unlike the ones that floated down the Nile,
This ship operates with a rudderless style. . .
It's a dictatorship.

The captain served his apprenticeship
As a horseman with no horsemanship
Yet his crew solidified their ridership
And questioned everyone else's citizenship

Gone are the days of bipartisanship
And back are the days of censorship
There will never be another legislatorship
For a dictatorship is a controllership

Self-elevated to a king or a monarchy,
He made democracy a thing of the past
After 236 years of liberty,
the outdated Constitution could not last

"The First Love Song"

The first love song coincided with the first broken heart.

It was probably composed at the beginning of time

by an early man to try and explain something that his heart couldn't comprehend.

While his mind composed the lyrics, his heart added the rhythmic beat using his whole body as the first human rhythm section,

and the first love song was born out of pain and loneliness.

If a heart was never broken then we wouldn't have a need for love songs.

Love songs are made for yesterday, today, and tomorrow to ensure that

we never forget how it truly feels to be in love.

The rapture and the ecstasy of first love combine

to create a one-of-a-kind experience never able to be duplicated by anyone or anything else.

The first love song was a gift to the world that affects all mankind.

It started out as a cry for understanding and led to a universal truth.

We are forever grateful to the poor soul who felt the first pain of love.

We pray that love songs continue to legislate our hearts and our lives.

Hopefully, the last love song has not been written yet
And there is still time to clear the air with much regret
It's hard to imagine a world where love has gone away for good
That would mean love was just a game that we never really understood.

"The Poetry Haters"

Please don't hate on things you don't understand
Poetry is a gift for the enlightened reader
A poet can lift the world with her hand
And function as your favorite cheerleader

Don't hate the poetry but you can hate the game
Poetry was made to glorify life's gifts
Reading poetry does not make you lame
And quite often your spirit it lifts

Poetry is not written for the faint of heart
But anyone can find pleasure in its verse
A poem a day provides a brand-new start
It's like poetic water to quench your thirst

People who read poetry are often smarter
They appreciate the rhythm and the rhyme
They enjoy their cup of poetic water
And realize that reading poetry is not a crime

"THE POLITICS OF LOVE"

If you vote for me, I'll vote for you
As long as I am the only candidate
Love can be the platform to see us through
And I will proudly serve as your running mate

We can remain in office for a lengthy term
For my only constituents are you and my heart
We will certify the ballots in order to confirm
That we won the campaign and will never depart

We will serve each other with truth to power
We will always be happy throughout our reign
Every day I will care for you just like a flower
And for me, I know you will do the same

Love and politics are not a universal match
But the politics of love is nothing new
Politicians turn their backs for you to scratch
Lovers prefer to have your back to keep their love true

"Time Capsule"

Poetry, both good and bad,

Is a thinking person's gift –

Poetry is also a reminder

That sometimes we need a lift –

Poetry offers us a better view

Of the poet's wisdom and life –

By reading about his private thoughts,

Lost loves and inner strife –

Hopefully, 100 years from now

These poems will still care –

Whether you took the time

To appreciate them but also to share –

Poetry should never be used

As a measurement of our wealth –

Yet, poetry can be used

As an engagement of our mental health –

I offer these poems to you

As a token of my admiration –

With no expectation attached

Other than your respect and your appreciation.

"TOUCH"

Why do lovers hold hands?
Why do lovers kiss?
True love makes no demands
And real love is hard to resist

A budding romance may start with a glance, but it's the holding of hands
that leads to the kissing of lips that seals the deal.

Holding hands with the one you love is the oldest example of
non-verbal communication there is that actually connects human souls.

Like connecting both the positive and negative ends to a battery,
the two hands ignite a spark that runs through both bodies
to electrify their spirits as long as the hands are touching.

It is the most indescribable feeling to walk hand-in-hand
with the one you love on a sunny day while smiling at the sun,
or on a starry night while gazing at the moon.

Humans touching humans fortify a lifelong connection that needs no
words.
The touching implies that words are not necessary to communicate
the love between the two.

Those who are blind or deaf also get to enjoy and experience
the same feeling of touch when holding hands or kissing lips.

Clasping hands to be safe and warm
Two aged lovers crossed the street
Protecting each other from life's harm
Then they kissed to make life complete

"VANITY"

Even her birth was one of vanity
Born in a bed with a huge canopy
Being vain is a common weakness
The exact opposite of one with meekness

It is the scourge of all humanity
And morally undesired like profanity
Vanity's close friend is too much pride
They travel together on a Ferris Wheel ride

If the meek will indeed inherit the Earth
Then being vain is not what it's worth
Vanity is widely considered a deadly sin
There's no way for vain people to ever win

Vanity often begins with a false belief
It's really no more than a common thief
Vanity will not bring you lasting wealth
The diagnosis for it is still mental health

The vanity craze is a worthless trip
A Titanic ride on a sinking ship
Check yourself before it's too late
Look in the mirror you are overweight

"THE KNEE GROWS"

Once upon a time I fell and bumped my knee.
Soon, the knee turned big and black and
It began to bother me;

I pampered it and rubbed it and kissed it
And everything, but it wouldn't stop swelling.
The more I rubbed it, the more it swelled.

It suddenly dawned on me that maybe I had
rubbed it the wrong way. I realize now that
no matter what I do, the knee grows…

"THE DOWNERS GROUND"

At Montana Street Elementary School,

there was an infamous spot on the playground

that all the kids referred to as the Downers Ground.

It was a sandbox-like area that was ruled by bullies

and such like big Rudy Lewis who had a rough touch.

With swing sets, sliding boards and monkey bars

nearby, the Downers Ground was a spot to beware.

Some kids played the dozen to taunt Rudy,

and the next thing we saw was them flying

in the air and landing on their booty.

A few kids got really hurt and never returned

to the playground. The principal and teachers

were aware but even they avoided the Downers Ground.

Elementary students can sometimes be cruel

and easily forget the Golden Rule.

Girls and boys alike would often take

flight on the Downers Ground.

But one day Big Rudy met his match

and tried to down tall Virgil Grace.

It surprised us all when Rudy was the one

who ended up on his face.

Rudy was big and slow and Virgil was

fast and tall which made it more difficult

for Virgil to fall.

After that, the Downers Ground was not the same

and we all decided to change its name.

Although it was still the same old place,

Rudy was eliminated by a Fall from Grace.

"Sun/Son"

The Sun —
That great ball of fire that
The Earth revolves around
Mandates the changing of the guard.

My Son –
Reminds me of that sun
As I revolve around him
Like a lighthouse beacon.

The Sun –
Lights the way for us to see
Providing energy for all;
We cannot live without its warmth.

My Son –
Sees the way lit for him
And follows like a leader
Destined to bask in his own glow.

"STICK"

Sticktoitiveness
is an informal term that means
having a fierce tenacity – staying together, like:
> In sickness and in health
> Til death do us part

We all desire someone who knows how to stick,
a mate that will be with us forever like:
> A soulmate.

And likewise, we need to also have that
> Sticktoitiveness

In order to remain together with that mate.
Today, jumping ship is too easy to do
when faced with troubled waters.
But we all know that still waters run deep
And even deeper if the love is true and sincere.
In a world where blood is supposed to be
> thicker than water,

I choose you to be my mate in life
> and I promise to always stick.

"SPARKLES"

Gold glitters and sparkles
　　　　by nature
But friendships have to be
　　　　nurtured before they can sparkle.

My knowledge of gold jewelry
　　　　and other precious metals
is very limited. I can't tell
　　　　fine jewelry from Fool's Gold.

But my knowledge of friendships formed
　　　　with Trust and Love is more precious
than any precious metals.

Everyone knows that gold sparkles,
　　　　diamonds sparkle, sugar sparkles,
glass sparkles, and sometimes even Unicorns
　　　　sparkle. Although each is very special,
I'd rather see your eyes sparkle with love for me.

Things of Gold
　　　　are very precious
to those who care
　　　　to collect them.

Friends of Old

       are very precious

to those who dare

       not forget them.

My eyes will always sparkle for you.

"SOUTHERN-FRIED POETRY"

Down South, everything we ate was usually fried
It was the most delicious food you ever tried
     Yes, some places even served fried rattlesnake
     No, what you just read was not a mistake

The mouth of the South is an incredibly voracious beast
Everything we eat is a heavenly fried feast
     I was raised on fried chicken, fried tomatoes, fried corn
     We were fed fried foods as soon as the day we were born

Fried eggs, fried okra, fried peanuts, and fried ham
We even had fried ice cream, fried donuts, and fried Spam
     Apple fritters, funnel cakes, and turkey were all fried
     We'd never heard of cholesterol so no one ever died

French fries, fried green beans, and fried yams
Were favorites that always made us say, "Thank you, ma'am"
     When our parents would shop at the local grocery
     They'd buy all the things that became southern-fried poetry

Dieters, vegans and vegetarians should all beware
Visit down South only if you are brave enough to dare
     Grits, oatmeal, and cream-of-wheat are still protected
     Only because we're unsure how frying will make them digested

So, tell everyone you know that southern-fried love is the best
A Southerner's stomach comes first to put him to the test
        We will never abandon the things that make us who we are
        Southern fried foods are common to us and not so bazaar

"Sooner or Later"

Dessert usually comes after dinner, but I want mine before

Saving you for later would be too much of a tease

If we start now, we can finally settle the score

As to who will get there first and the last to cry, "Please"

Later is for losers and I would rather always win

Second best for the game we play is pretty good

Being first is the goal as long as you tell me when

It's important for us not to be misunderstood

Neighbors who eavesdrop will not spoil our fun

Listening so close to each and every gasp

We'll let them all know that you are the one

And our love will never be found in a looking glass

"CADILLACS IN MY EYES"

If girls were cars in the 1970s, she'd be a Cadillac
The flagship of all high-class models to beat
I didn't know how to drive then and that's a fact
But I could see that she had a nice body and a very soft seat

After seeing her, I had Cadillacs in my eyes
And she was my favorite brand of transportation
She transported me through the clouds and the skies
I averaged fifty smiles per gallon at her filling station

Cruising with her gave driving a whole new meaning
I sometimes put her in reverse so that I could parallel park
I admired her wheels and roomy trunk when I was cleaning
We cruised in the moonlight on the avenue until dark

Cars and girls were made for each other
I love hot rods and luxury cars alike
Convertible tops with big headlights make the best lovers
I'd rather ride her any day than ride my bike

"ONA"

Her name was Ona for short and she was
  Also, very pretty and smart, but proud and free

I met her fully in the summer at college
  And I lost her completely by winter semester

But I never forgot her
  Even the letters of her unique name

Remind me of what we once had
  O-N-A wherever you are, I still care

But why did it have to be a One Night Affair?

"OLD SCHOOL LOVE"

Gave her a dozen red roses
> With a Hallmark card

Took her to a nice dinner
> And then to a two-dollar movie

Popcorn, drinks, and chocolate candy bars
> Held hands with interlocked fingers

Smooched during the movie trailers
> Laid her head softly on my shoulders

Opened the door for her and walked her home
> Stood very close to her under the porch light

Pecked her on the jaw for a kiss on a first date
> Went home and dreamed about her all nightlong

"LOVE ON A BUDGET"

I can't afford to spread my love all over town

     My finances and my heart are not that rich

Maybe I can do a matinee and a blue plate special

     I don't have much scratch but I do have an itch

"MAGIC IS AS MAGIC DOES"

A musician is a magician with every performance
        A hairstylist performs magic with each new hairdo

A pilot is a magician any time a plane safely lands
        When a doctor delivers a baby, it's magic

A magic spell is cast when two people fall in love
        It's magic when a tree sprouts a tiny twig overnight

Magic is as magic does whether we believe in magic or not
        I believe magic is that which makes this world seems real

"Mustard Seed Poetry"

tiny but mighty
is the significance
of the mustard seed metaphor

as humans we are already small
but once we lose our faith
we continue to grow smaller

mustard seeds grow larger
because they keep their faith

they believe in the power
of strength through growth

a big person can have
a small amount of faith

a small person can have
a large amount of faith

size only matters when
it comes to personal salvation

the faith of a mustard seed
is what is required to grow
e x p o n e n t i a l l y

"PEOPLE ARE CHRISTMAS, TOO"

Who said Christmas only comes from a store

All neatly wrapped with a bow and nestled under a tree?

Our parents, siblings, friends, and loved ones

Everywhere are all Christmas, too.

For the true gift we share is the Love,

Peace, and the Happiness.

Not just with our loved ones

But with people everywhere.

Nothing could mean more at Christmas

Than loving each other and our neighbors

Because we are Christmas, too.

"SHACK'S GRILL CAFÉ

Nickel jukebox in the southwest corner
Bluesman B.B. King playing with Lucille
Stinky chitlins cooking in the kitchen
Folks fighting to get inside Shack's Grill.

Shack chewing on his Hav-A-Tampa cigar
Kiss Pig sitting outside on the stoop
Smoking inside and dancing in the back
Tables jam-packed with the usual group.

Fried fish and barbecue are not on the menu
Candy, gum, and cigarettes behind the counter
Oysters on the half shell with hot sauce is new
If trouble starts, Shack serves as the bouncer

Burgers, dogs, beer and liquor
But no telephone or TV to see
Shack's Grill is now gone for good
And all I have is my memory.

"SCIENCE-BASED POETRY"

Seven planets briefly aligned in the night sky;
they created what some call a planetary parade.

Only five planets were visible with the naked eye;
the other two were too far to be displayed.

Mercury is the smallest but closest to the sun;
known as the swiftest planet, it is pretty fast.

Venus is the hottest and the second from the sun;
spins clockwise on its axis and is part of the cast.

Mars, the orange-red planet covered in iron oxide dust;
the fourth planet from the sun is one of the brightest.

Jupiter is the largest planet and it doesn't have a crust;
made of swirling gases and liquids, it may be the lightest.

Saturn is a gas giant with a distinctive ring;
it has 62 moons and is constantly spinning.

Neptune is not easily visible but is a massive thing;
even using telescopes makes Neptune very challenging.

Uranus, a blue-colored ice giant made of water and methane;
it has the lowest temperature of all and is very complex.

A planetary parade is rare but easy to explain;
What will the world's scientists think up next?

"A Stacked Deck"

A lovely goddess floating on celestial air
Beautiful hair flowing without an earthly care
He saw her walk by with a pretty stacked deck
Three tens and four aces all below her neck

He quickly shuffled his cards to make her stay
But she was too slick at the game for her to play
He cut the cards to further ignite a fiery flame
She noticed his attraction and decided to play his game

With a poker face and a full house, she dealt him a card
His royal flush made her blush as he threw down real hard
He won the first round by bending all the rules
He suspected she was used to playing with silly old fools

Card sharps know how to really shuffle a deck
The stakes were so high she had to write a check
He covered her check and countered her bet
He promised her a game that she would never forget

Her confidence cooled when she realized his skill
If his cards didn't win the game, his good looks will
When it was time for them to make the final play
He won the game, her, and together they walked away

"Kiss From A Rose"

It all started with a kiss.

      A kiss to a Rose and

      a kiss from a Rose

      happened at my college

      in the mid-1970s.

Two Roses held hands and kissed after a game
underneath the bleachers at the baseball stadium.

Rose Brown and Rose White were star athletes
who longed to *Come Out* but were afraid of the backlash.

LGBTQ was not yet widely acknowledged and
prejudice precluded a white rose from
kissing a brown rose in public.

It may have started with a kiss
but it continued with so much more.
When the rest of the team found out,
they quietly put pressure on the two to stop it.

Unwittingly, they targeted Rose Brown
as the initiator and tried to force her
off the team with *Let's Get Brown To Quit.*

And that was the first time we heard the letters
L G B T Q together.

"HALF-BAKED POETRY"

As a poet, I have composed many poems

That I initially thought were half-baked

Or not yet ready for primetime publication.

I felt they were either too short, too long,

Or too abstract.

Yet, I set them free anyway because

That's what my muse urged me to do

At the time.

The boundary of poetry is pretty wide:

The shortest poem in history

Was recorded as only containing two words.

And the longest poem ever written contained

1.8 million words, an epic poem from India

With over 200,000 lines long.

My poetry is not as short or as long as the

Examples stated, but like every other normal poet,

Mine is somewhere in between.

The point is: Half-baked poetry may not taste

As good as a half-baked cookie but its purpose

Is to communicate, not to necessarily taste good.

"GRAFFITI"

In school, on all the walls, our names were scribbled like graffiti
Declaring our love for each other so the whole world could truly see
We were too young to know that our love would not last
And our names would someday be erased and considered part of the past

Graffiti is for the young trying to figure out who they are
Painted names on buildings belong with the days of the streetcar
As the artists' age, the paint fades to reveal their immaturity
They can no longer remember why they wrote such words with such urgency

When cave men wrote on walls, it was not called graffiti
It was the dawning of an age when ideas were trying to be free
That freedom led to communication, education, and business marketing
Modern day advertising has now become an everyday offering

Some of our cities have gotten real smart
They figured out how to turn graffiti into beautiful art
No longer considered an eyesore or even blight
The work generated by graffiti artists is intended to excite

Creativity is the spark that urges some to deface
True art is that which should never be erased
Graffiti does not ensure a place in history
But it does help define the lost art mystery

Poetry on walls in public bathrooms is everywhere

With the ink now dried, no one seems to care

Graffiti can be art if done to look professionally

Beauty is in the eye of the beholder and always will be

"CONFLICTION"

When I was young, I fell in love with my babysitter. She was 18 and I was 10. At night when she tucked me in, her breasts touched my face as she kissed my forehead and I got aroused below my waist. I couldn't understand what was happening to me. I was conflicted.

In high school, I learned that my parents were divorcing. My dad moved to the basement and my mom stayed in the master bedroom, alone. They lived separate lives while living in the same house. Yet, my dad still attended all my games and my mom continued to cook family meals. Things stayed that way for years until my dad was found dead in the basement, alone. I couldn't comprehend what happened and I could not cry at his funeral.

One day in college I found a love letter inside my English book addressed to me. The author confessed their love for me and inquired if I felt the same way. The confessor was my English professor and he was a gay man. My stellar grade dramatically changed when I could not endorse his query. Because I never had those kinds of feelings for someone of the same sex, I was confused and wondered, "Why Me?"

When my wife and I married, we said our wedding vows facing each other and pledged to stay together in sickness and in health until death do us part. The death of our marriage came early and only lasted a year when we found ourselves in divorce. I vowed never to marry again because I didn't comprehend what happened before.

Confliction is a real thing and it can happen to anyone at anytime, anywhere. I was even conflicted about writing this, but then I realized that understanding is the real antidote. I hope that my confliction will help someone else who also may have been conflicted at times. Confliction does not have to be a lifelong addiction if we learn how to validate and address our fears.

"PROVERBS 2025"

A bridge over troubled waters can be a welcomed relief
But not so much to those who are living underneath

Raindrops keep falling on your head
Because you chose to stay out in the rain instead

A penny saved is a penny worth earning
Except when we spend it all because our pockets are burning

Beauty is only skin deep is often true
If you're not too vain to see the real you

When we fall down, we should get up again
To show the world that we intend to win

Ain't no sunshine since she's been gone
Because the moon switched places with the dawn

A lover's stitch in time saves nine
Especially when the love you save is mine

When bad is good and good is bad
It's probably the best that you ever had

Early to bed, early to rise
Means you spent the night in paradise

The grass is not necessarily greener on the other side
Unless you actually reside on the other side

"QUIET POETRY"

Poetry

is not meant to be quiet.

Its purposefulness is to excite

and enliven the soul with

boundless faith, hope, and love.

Poetry

loves those who love it back.

Some fail to understand or appreciate

it's subtlety or it's gravity, but it will always exist.

Poetry

begs the questions and simultaneously

gives us the answers our lives crave.

Life is like a long poem within a maze

of poetic expressions.

Poetry

is the rhythm of night trains

and noisy trucks on busy highways

that wind through neighborhoods

with laughing children on swing sets.

Poetry

presents our world endless possibilities

to believe in parallel worlds and

alternate universes of intelligence

through earthly books.

Poetry
lulls us to sleep only to
awaken our Innervisions
with lush memories of
days gone by and dreams of tomorrow.

"Phobias"

I have a fear of convertible cars, motorcycles, and sleeping outdoors.

Ever since the assassination of President John Kennedy on television, I have never wanted to ride in a convertible, much less own or even rent one.

My phobia of being in an unprotected wide-open space somehow transferred over to motorcycles and sleeping outdoors without a tent or covering surrounding me.

While others may fear airplanes, guns, snakes, spiders, worms, and such, I don't get spooked around them.

Some people laugh when they hear about my phobias and think I am being eccentric, but I'm not.

When I hear of others who are afraid of clowns, witches, water, cats, and mice, I think they are the ones who are eccentric.

Different strokes for different folks, I guess.

Let me be clear: I don't get panic attacks and I am not mortally afraid of convertibles, motorcycles, or sleeping outdoors.

I can certainly be around them with no problems, but I choose not to ride in a convertible, on a motorcycle, or sleep in the open outdoors without an enclosure.

I'm also not an extreme claustrophobic, but I get very uncomfortable lying prone in a coffin-like MRI machine for 45 minutes without being able to scratch my forehead.

I was not scarred by being in law enforcement and carrying a gun for 23 years; I felt that was in the line of my duty.

However, the three things I define as what I least like have never been a part of my line of duty or scope of employment.

I am an extrovert, a writer, an actor, and much more with some added baggage that I'm not proud of, but that's who I am.

Any person who does not have any phobias may be the person you should be concerned about the most.

"PHILLY CHEESESTEAK"

I've lived in Philly for almost 30 years
and never had a cheesesteak
Yet, I went to a Cheesecake Factory
recently and had some cheesecake

I don't really like cheese
and I gave up eating beef and pork,
but cheesecake tastes so delicious
on the end of my lonely fork

Philly is famous for a lot of things
other than a cheesesteak sandwich
30th Street Station, the Rocky statue
and Philly Zoo, are examples of which

But all everyone remembers is
the Philly Cheesesteak made with Cheez Whiz
I even saw that featured on TV
during a Philadelphia Jeopardy quiz

Another famous relative of the cheesesteak
is the Philly Tasty Kake
They taste even better when
you can have them freshly baked

Philadelphia is known for
a lot of other good food
And everyone seems to love it
from a city slicker to a country dude

So, whenever you visit Philly,
please remember to take a break
in the City of Brotherly Love,
and fall in love with a Philly cheesesteak

"Making Love In Public"

Making love in public is not what you think
Sometimes it's just a look or maybe a blink

It has more to do with intimate secrecy
Than it does to do with public decency

It can happen up close or from a distance
It can happen anywhere without resistance

The birds and the bees started the fling
And created a naturally wonderful thing

Sometime later you may hear from the stork
Making a delivery that yet cannot walk

Any affection of public love is what we need now
It's okay to love without taking a vow

We should all make love so the public can see
That loving thy neighbor is the way nature planned it to be

"Milk of Magnesia"

America has been known

to sometimes eat its own

without the aid of milk of magnesia

and then conveniently develop mass amnesia

to somehow manage to forget all the carnage
and collateral damage.

"SNAKE OIL"

Standing on the corner and dressed to kill, he caught her eye.

He looked like a million dollars and she bought everything he was selling.

Unbeknownst to her, he was a snake oil salesman on the sly.

She was blinded by the gold dust in her eyes and the lies he was telling.

Everything that shines is not gold is what the old folks say.

The brain should be the thermostat for the heart.

But Fool's Gold tends to dull the senses and runs common sense away.

All in love might be fair but no one ever said all in love is smart.

Many buy things they don't need or even want to prove a point.

Buyer's remorse is when one is unable to return what was purchased in haste.

The return policy on love and affection is something one cannot usually flaunt.

At the end of the day, all the time spent flaunting mostly turns to waste.

Snake oil is a fraudulent, cure-all elixir sold by those who are slick.

Lies, promises, and too-good-to-be-true guarantees can be similar.

In order to unmask a fraud, one has to be nimble and quick.

Instead of being tricked by the smoke and mirrors, learn to be a good listener.

Snake oil can't sell itself and often needs a purveyor.

When things are not what they appear to be, look closer at the source.

It's a good bet that the slickster is dishonest and a betrayer.

But remember, to purchase or not, is always your choice.

Snake oil is like a rabbit's foot which is an unlucky charm,

Both have to be dead to make your fortunes come true.

Superstitious beliefs can cause a lot of harm

Unless one is smarter than the salesman who sells them to you.

Be careful about buying things you don't understand or know their worth.

The currency you use may not be eligible for a rebate.

Love is in this category and can often result in a new birth.

For gullible buyers are too much in a hurry to wait.

A final warning to all who sell or use snake oil just for fun.

Clearly, this is something that you should not practice or ever do.

Because the frequent use of snake oil might not be able to be undone.

And at the end of the day, the snake is transformed into you.

"SAMSON & DELILAH"

Samson, a shaggy-haired mutt
fell in love with Delilah,
a prim and proper Chihuahua.

When he tried to propose,
she turned up her nose
and acted like she didn't see him;
After Samson's owners had him dipped and clipped,
everyone was in awe.

Instead of a mutt,
he looked regal like King Tut
and Delilah changed her mind on a whim.
Every day they wanted to play
and sniff each other all over;

It wasn't long when love
started playing their song
and marriage was on its way.

Samson let his hair grow back
and they set the date for October;
Delilah gained weight because she
couldn't wait until their wedding day.

As they walked down the aisle,
everyone started to smile
at their adorable look.
Samson looked big and strong
but all along he was still a mutt.

Delilah had gained a few pounds
and was sort of round,
but still had her hook.

Samson and Delilah
were married that day
and walked away
with a canine strut.

"ANOTHER SOLO"

Life is a medley of songs sung in various keys
Usually performed by a choir, but sometimes solos are required;
The solos for gospel hymns and love songs are examples of these
Yet, there are other kinds of solos that help us to stay inspired.

A solo of independence is usually the first song we sing
To declare the initiative to forge our self-identity;
The melody we choose helps to determine the lyrics we bring
And make us who we are throughout life's eternity.

Everyone has to sing solo once in a while
And take their turn in the symphony of sharing
Singing solo and being solo is quite versatile
And standing out front of everyone is bold and daring

Life is a solo worth singing:

> No matter how empty and remote
> Life makes you feel at times,
> Always look for a brighter day.
> For the peace withing yourself
> Makes all of life's ups and downs
> Worth living through.

And remember, sometimes even

> Counselors need counsel-ing
> Preachers need preach-ing,
> Doctors need doctor-ing
> And poets need poet-ing.

"Never Give Up"

When death comes first and life hasn't a chance to enter,

There's no Fall, Summer, or Spring – only Winter

Darkness covers darkness with more darkness

Your eyes will never have the chance to witness

Giving up is never really a good idea

It's always better to believe that hope will appear

Death before life should not be an obsession

Especially when life is your God-given possession

Oftentimes life is hard and difficult to bear

Failure is not inevitable just because doubt is everywhere

Know that a silver lining is just around the bend

Life belongs to you but it's not really yours to end

Giving up and letting go should not be your only choices

If so then you are likely listening to the wrong voices

I beg you to reconsider your valuable worth

Your life is important and it matters here on this Earth

Like an ill-fated star never given the chance to twinkle,

Your dreams will be suspended in time like Rip Van Winkle

Love conquers all is a misunderstood cliché at its best

For death conquers all and love conquers the rest

"Sky Dancing"

If clouds can dance, so can I
Something happens to me when I see your face
My mind and body take flight and float real high
My feet leave the ground and head toward space

I dance across the sky like Fred Astaire
Without fear of those who make fun of me
Because love takes over and controls the air
My shoes are magic and my soul is free

A happy heart with happy feet is at play
I will never ever be the same
The birds and the bees watch my ballet
I am electric without any shame

I dance all day and dream all night
Never missing a beat when you are near
For you are the reason my love is in flight
And the one who makes my love sincere

I never learned to dance when I was on Earth
My two left feet were so uncoordinated
But my whole world changed upon your birth
And now I am so glad that I waited

Sky Dancing is the way you make me feel
And it's something I will never regret
I know true love and this love is real
Up there, I rejoice the day that we finally met

"PREMATURE"

My eyes sized her up too fast
My heart allowed her in too soon
What I felt initially would not last
My mind was hypnotized by the moon

Her touch deactivated my force-field
Her kiss short-circuited my energy
My defenses were no longer a shield
That's the reason for this eulogy

Premature activation is a common fault
It always makes us jump the gun
I should have kept my love in the vault
And let time reveal she was the one

"PLAYING MY OLD SCHOOL MUSIC JUST FOR YOU"

As I sit before the keyboard of my favorite instrument,
        I prepare to do a song just for you.

It doesn't really matter which key I strike,
        For the tune still comes out the same.

I'm only playing to an audience of one
        So, forget about the encores and standing ovations.

The only standing ovation I need
        Is for you to forever stand by me.

And if for some reason, you ever tire of hearing me
        Bang on my keyboard, just tell me.

I'll put away my typewriter and sing for you instead.

"HALO"

A halo is a circle of light above an angel's head

The sun is a circle of light that warms our lives

The moon is a circle of light that shades our love

A star is a circle of light that grants our wishes

Love is a circle of light that shines in our heart

My heart is a circle of light that shines for you

Your eyes are circles of light that dim the angel's halo

The sun, moon and stars combined cannot outshine all the love in my heart that I feel for you

I love you with all my soul and if I had things my way,

I'd wear your love as a halo above my head.

"Heaven Eyes"

Heaven Eyes
With foxy thighs
And a magnificent personality.
Cause me to see pearly gates down here
And forget the ones I'll never see.

Heaven Eyes
To my surprise
Is a down-to-earth reality.
If her sweet sensation can bring salvation
Then in her arms is the place for me.

Heaven Eyes
They all despise
Her sexy femininity.
But they would all give rather than receive
An arm for her beauty.

Heaven Eyes
She's no jive
Or artificiality.
She's no savior but her behavior
Is so divine to me.

"Her Comb, My Brush"

She combed her hair
And I brushed mine
We're such a lovely pair

Her hair was long
And mine was short
Our love was very strong

We were too excited
And anxious to wed
All our friends were invited

Our wedding day's here
Walk down the aisle
Golden rings bright and clear

We combed through life
With life's bristled brush
She became my faithful wife

Her comb, my brush
What an unbeatable pair
We are a royal flush

"When Love Wasn't Enough"

I adored my best friend
We loved each other throughout grade school
Daily love notes we used to send
For loving her was my golden rule

After school we hit a rough patch
But we stayed together through it all
I never regretted our love match
Even when the bridge started to fall

It seems love's glue wasn't enough
We couldn't save us from ourselves
Our separation was really tough
We both drifted to someone else

Years passed by and I didn't see her
But my heart still reminisced
The way it was and the way we were
Until the day of our final kiss

"White Coat Syndrome"

Afraid of doctor's offices, he never went
He believed all cures were heaven sent
His first doctor visit was at ninety-three
He was so old then he could hardly see

He heard the doctor say he had Cadillacs in his eyes
He was almost blind but still considered himself wise
His wife had died so he was able to outlive her
But the doctor also diagnosed him with a ferocious liver

Homemade remedies always saw him through
He always knew exactly what to do
He had a cure for every infirmity
Herbs, soups, and salves were all usually key

At 93, he was too far gone for any of them
His whole lungs were filled with heavy phlegm
The x-rays showed a huge inner mass
The hospital believed that he wouldn't last

Born at home and delivered by midwife
He had never really gone under the knife
The doctor wanted to remove his cancer
Of course, a belligerent "No" was his answer

He went home and boiled a pot of mystical stew

Set out to prove that the doctor's theory was untrue

He surprised the doctor when he walked through the door

A year later when he had just turned ninety-four

"WE 3 KINGS"

We three kings of Southern Charm
The three cash crops we chose to farm:
Cotton, peanuts, and the pecan
Is how our fortunes all began

King cotton was the first to be crowned
He made our city world renowned
Its snow-white crown above the crowd
In order to pick, you must be bowed

The King of peanuts saved our land
This farming miracle started by one man
Dr. Carver, a former-slave-turned-scientist
Without him, this cash crop would not exist

King pecan was the heir to our wealth
Its nutritious longevity aided our health
Sales are still strong to this very day
Pecans are the ones still paving the way

Cotton, peanuts, and the pecan
Is how our fortunes all began
Each one a bountiful cash crop
These three kings remain at the top

(These are the three staple crops of Dothan, Alabama)

"YOU MAKE ME . . . "

Like water trickling down a stream,
   YOU MAKE ME LAUGH.

Like a flame fluttering on a candle,
   YOU MAKE ME FEEL HAPPY.

Like a flower blooming in sunshine,
   YOU MAKE ME FEEL WARM.

Like a mirage appearing in a desert,
   YOU MAKE ME FEEL UNLONELY.

Like a targeted Cupid's arrow,
   YOU MAKE ME FEEL LOVED.

Like a child sliding down a snowy hill.
   YOU MAKE MY LIFE FUN.

"A Yellow-Bellied Sapsucker"

The first fight I ever had

was when I was in the eighth grade.

A classmate, in an effort to curse me

out by saying I was a coward,

called me a Yellow-bellied Sapsucker

to try and get under my skin; I didn't bite.

Then he dared me to knock

a piece of wood off his shoulder;

I thought that was stupid too and refused.

He pushed me in my chest

and proceeded to wrestle with me.

We rumbled across the gym floor

like drunken ballet dancers.

He swung at me and I ducked;

I swung at him and he ducked.

No punches ever connected and

then someone broke us apart.

Neither one of us won the fight,

but as my foe angrily walked away,

he turned and yelled a refrain:

"You Yellow-bellied Sapsucker!"

And I shot him a bird.

"The Soul of an Enigma"

Mystery shrouds the face behind his immortal mask;
His moon-set eyes glimmer away in search of a virgin horizon.
> Both calm and disquieting, his body is a winding road that
Zig-zags between the limitations of life,
> And chaperones his heart throughout the dances with love.

Self-made riddles of his world flutter those hearts
> Who do not see past his smiling windows.
Man, or more, he readily provokes wonder in search of
> The key to his obscurity.
He is truly an enigma to many.

To him day and night are the same
> When perception is attached to the retina.
The mind encodes the message to the coy puzzle and
> Love pierces the heart of the decoder.
His restless soul dances with his imagination and ours.

"Walk Right Up To The Moon"

With my heart filled full of love,
We walked right up to the moon.
The only thing I was thinking of
Was the day we wed in June.

Confident that my life was on point,
I planned to live forever after with her.
We were matched perfectly during our anoint
And the preacher blessed our rings to concur.

I planned to never again stray away
From the love and duty I pledged.
There would never be another play
Regardless of what others have alleged.

Paradise on the moon collided with the sun
And clouded our marital bliss with rain.
Our tears streamed down when love was undone
We couldn't escape the misery and the pain.

Walking up to the moon was our mistake
For we never considered the aftermath.
The flowers withered and so did the cake
Our feet now traveled two separate paths.

Our love was ended without a pun
We should have listened closer to the song.
For walking right up to the sun
Was where we should have gone.

(Based on the song "Walk Right Up to the Sun" by The Delfonics)

"The Sound of Harps"

Often played by Cherubs,

The harp is heaven's piano;

Heaven knows harps are for lovers

And designed the harp to sound like:

Angels playing heaven's piano

Cupid plucking his bow and arrow

Cherubs giggling in the wind

Rain falling playfully on a tin roof

"VOLCANIC ERUPTIONS"

He was both homely and lonely
until he met a girl his equal.
She appeared to be hot and lit
the pilot light to his cold-furnace heart,
And the two of them loved like regular people.
She caused his thermostat to reset to a brand-new start.

It wasn't long before he noticed
a non-seasonal temperature change.
Her face turned red like a hot volcano
and her actions became hard to explain;
Their love would never be the same.

Her disruption spewed lava-like pain
that consumed his body and the town.
Her affection transferred from heat into hate,
and true love was nowhere to be found.
When the volcano erupted, their fate was too late.

Warning, never fall in love with
a smoldering volcano if you can help it.
Both male or female are the same difference.
The hole where their heart should be
is a deep, miserable pit.

Volcanic ash leaves an unforgettable residue.

Your body can forgive but your mind will never forget.

Age-old lessons and sage advice always ring true.

When they erupt, volcanoes are a life-altering threat.

A quiet volcano should be respected from a safe distance

and the power they hold must be revered.
Don't be fooled by their harmless appearance.
As a reminder, this final warning should always be adhered.

"WHAT ARE BOYS MADE OF?"

Snakes, snails, and puppy dog tails
Are what occupy boys' dreams;
Boys are naturally curious
As they try to figure out things like
Dogs, cars, kites, drums,
Mud, frogs, school and girls.

Their heads are just right for
Birthday hats and their fingers
Are perfect for ripping open presents.
May all your birthday dreams come true
As you blow out the candles on your cake.

"EVERYTHING NICE"

(What Girls Are Made Of)

Sugar, spice and everything nice

Are what girls are made of

But girls are also made of

Ice cream, cake, pink ribbons,

yellow dresses, furry kittens,

silly giggles, sweet kisses,

jump ropes, baby dolls

and happy birthdays

Here's wishing all girls more

of Everything Nice!

"FOR DR. MAYA ANGELOU, PH.D."

(aka Marguerite Johnson, 1928-2014)

Poet.
        Dancer.
Singer.
        Author.
Activist.
        Hero.
Angel.
        Indelible life.
Outstanding literary works.
        Phenomenal woman.

She knew why the caged bird sings
        Because she was once a caged bird.

Her innocence was stolen at the young age of seven
        When someone ruffled her feathers

And entered her cage – to deflower her.
        Afterwards, her voice was muted for five years.

This silence within allowed her to hone
        Her super powers of extraordinary observation
And listening through her love of words, books,
        And a high-powered imagination fueled by self-rediscovery.

Her dreams reimagined a world where her writings became the gold standard

>> And everyone else wanted to emulate her freedom

To sing her own songs in her own voice

>> Without the muffling of other outside forces,

No matter how much they tried to influence or dissuade her.

>> She poetically danced and sang her way through a Jim Crow world

That she reauthored with six volumes of her own memoirs

>> That turned her into an activist, a hero, and a subsequent angel.

She believed that humans are more alike than unalike

>> And even in death, she continues her rise to locate a more direct way

>> Into the soul's search for divine freedom.

Yes, she was once a caged bird on many levels, but she refused to be defined by those cages.

In retrospect, she thrived on her zest for life

>> As she continued to rise and thrive beyond the cages that failed to keep her imprisoned.

By any measure, Dr. Maya Angelou was a phenomenal woman who lived a phenomenal life filled with phenomenal praise.

>> And we will always hear the songs of the uncaged bird in the distant winds of the future on the pulse of every morning.

"Gil Scott-Heron's Voice"
(aka Gilbert Scott-Heron, April 1, 1949 – May 27, 2011)

I didn't know Gil Scott-Heron – personally
but I knew his voice – musically
What an unmistakable choice
to lead a revolution that was not
supposed to be televised all over the world.
He was no April Fool!
Chicago born. The Bronx raised. College educated. Folk Hero.

Spoken Word Music legend. The original Winter in America Soldier.

Never pretentious. A master of Reverse Psychology.

When he said, *The Revolution Will Not Be Televised,*
he was talking about the revolution of the mind as the real starting place,
but he also knew that the cameras would record his concerts
and document his revolutionary lifestyle.

We have the video footage to prove it.

Angel Dust... B-Movie... Johannesburg... all Pieces of a Man!
He was a Bluesologist, a Poet, an Author, an Icon.
Unfortunately, he surrendered to the pressures
and demons he so often warned others about
through his music.
Like Marvin Gaye before him, his soul was divided, but his
music like *"The Bottle"* and his voice will never be forgotten.
The Revolution *was* televised in real time. His revolution.

R.I.P. G.S.H.

"Hummingbirds"

Hummingbirds are really slumming birds
because they float around all summer long

They come in various colors
and they're not very tall

They chirp, they buzz, and they squeak
but they don't sing a song

Hummingbirds are unequivocally
the greatest birds of them all

Hummingbirds can't sing and they also don't cry
Their voice boxes are too tiny and they'd rather smile

They love to drink nectar from flowers nearby
It's always good to see them when they linger for awhile

Fireflies and hummingbirds are my favorite winged creatures
They symbolize Hope and Freedom when they enter our lives

Tiny but mighty and endowed with heavenly features
Their only rival might be equally wonderful butterflies

"A PARALLEL LOVE"

Some folks believe it's not possible to love two things
at different places in space and time,
> but I beg to differ.

I can't prove that parallel worlds exist,
but I can remember the time I first fell in love
and my heart is still tender.
That time and space may be illusive
> but the memory is very clear.

How many people love the Lord in Heaven
whom they have never seen
but feel every day through
> His divine presence?

Heaven is a real place in time and space
that exists in a parallel world
but yet we have to wait for
> the invitation to travel there.

"A PERFECT TOUCH"

A perfect touch
Is when you sneak into my daydream by secretly planting a seed,
Or when I cause you to desire me by superseding a previous need.
It's when I anticipate your phone call and then the phone rings
Or when you make all the right moves by saying all the right things.
A perfect touch
Is more spiritual than physical
It's actually what made Midas a miracle
A perfect touch
Is the way I smile when You think of Me
It's having the real thing, the perfect chemistry
Many could never understand this concept we're suggesting
Because they've never been touched by the spells we're casting
Sometimes love has a way of saying more than realized
And only those in love can truly recognize the disguise
You can still be my Secret Love if you want to be
And I will be patient and wait until you are free
As long as you know we'll never be the same
Until we really touch each other and give it a proper name

"A BLUE NOTE"

Is a blue note:

    A sad tune of loneliness?

A scribbled piece of paper?

    A romantic Soul Singer?

Whichever – They all remind me of how much I miss you.

    I guess you really *BLUE* my mind!

"BIG WORD POETRY"

I love your fluorescent, effervescent smile
And your taciturn acquiescence
            to my touch.

Your body relinquishes itself
To tempestuous emotions that can only be
            quenched with compliance.

When we are apart, a poignant foreboding
Pierces my heart to succumb to a panic
            of love lost forever.

When we are together, my mind traverses
across the celestial clouds to thank heaven
            for my kindred spirit.

Our love remains mellifluous but never nefarious
Because it is opulent and quintessential
            to who we were made to be.

If what we have turns out to be ephemeral,
My life would go into a downward spiral
            and meet a pernicious termination.

"BIRTHDAYS "

Birthdays are like butterflies,

they come and go on the wings of time

and leave us feeling blessed that

we got the chance to see another one.

Birthdays are also like rainbows,

they come rain or shine

and make us feel special that

they appeared just for us.

May you have the most wonderful birthday!

"But Wait. . . One More Thing!"

Late night talks on the telephone
We once talked for over five hours
Neither one of us wanted to be alone
The nighttime we claimed as all ours.

The things we discussed were very sublime
We talked about everything under the sun
We found each other at the right time
It became pretty clear that she was the one.

She had a beautiful smile and a pretty face
What we had was more than a simple fling
She tried to end the call with style and grace
I said, "But wait, I've got to say one more thing!"

We talked for another hour or two without end
I didn't want to let go and hang up the phone
Again, she tried to say, "Good night, my friend"
I panicked because I knew I would be alone.

She relented a little more and listened to me sing
My voice was not great but it kept her on the phone
And then she added, "But wait. . . one more thing!"
I knew then that she also did not want to be alone.

"ADDICTIONS "

A rich man gave up all his riches for it
A queen relinquished her throne to split
A preacher abandoned his lofty pulpit
An all-star pro athlete suddenly quit

The football player had a big concussion
His contract and career were up for discussion
He joined a rock band and played percussion
In between sets, he drank a White Russian

Left with no money he was faced with evictions
Jails are filled with pharmaceutical convictions
Once inside there are a multitude of restrictions
They are all designed to rehab the afflictions

The urge to own it beats all comprehension
It transfers the mind to a new dimension
It elevates the spirit to a high ascension
It manages to get the whole world's attention

An addiction can be a real game changer
It can transform one into an unknown stranger
Put the ones you love in fear and mortal danger
It can steal your life and make you a lone ranger

"CHOCOLATE NIGHTMARES"

Dark chocolate gives me wild nightmares.
I once dreamt I was covered in chocolate at birth–
And I could sense all the strange stares
As the doctors and nurses estimated my worth.

I was a chocolate baby with kinky hair.
My nose was broad and my lips were full –
I'd hoped that the world would be fair
Instead of being mean and cruel.

Chocolate is bad for you they say.
I say xenophobia makes you gain weight –
Calories from chocolate can burn away
But the weight of racism burns with hate.

I awoke to a milky white breakfast.
There was white bread and egg whites –
No more chocolate nightmares at last
I was back to normal without all the frights.

"Creaking Floors"

Home alone in an old home,
my creaking floors served as
a built-in alarm system
with no monthly fee.

The tiniest bit of pressure
from a cat or a dog would
set off a creaking noise
heard throughout the house.

Even a ghostly spirit
would be hard-pressed to
walk on these floors without
being eerily detected.

Strong winds and heavy rains
tend to cause the floors to
creak louder as if a spooky
haunting is taking place.

There's nothing like being
awakened from a sound sleep to
hear someone walking up the stairs
only to learn that it's the creaky floor.

"A Tropical Depression"

A tropical vacation is the ultimate place to be

Beautiful people as far as the human eye can see

I saw a tropical beauty sipping a pineapple-shaped drink made out of glass

Her dark curly hair made me wonder if she was also wearing a tropical skirt made of grass

When she arose, I saw the long grass skirt that clothed her figure

Tahitian dancers wear those when they dance, shaking their hips with so much vigor

I went to watch her dance at an outdoor theater

I was hoping to get a chance to talk to her later

There were many other beauties in the native dance troupe

But the one I liked stood out front and twirled a red hula hoop

She caught my eye as I stared at her with admiring delight

She smiled in my direction as her beautiful eyes beamed so bright

I smiled back at her being very careful not to show any teeth

Then I watched her grass skirt shake and shimmy beyond my belief

Her dancing aroused the crowd and definitely aroused me

My mind headed into a tropical fantasy away from all reality

Some guy behind me yelled "I love you honey!" and she waved her hand

I realized he had been the focus of her smile and he was her man

I felt so ashamed that I had gotten the wrong impression

I crashed back down to Earth into a tropical depression

I got so depressed that I wanted to run away and hide

My egotistical fantasy had taken me on a mistaken, tropical ride

"GENNY AND THE REV"

(The Marriage of Genesis to the Revelations)

Genny came first and The Rev came last.
They were married in the end to each other
And their ring was the circle called Earth.
That's the way it was meant to be
And that's the way it will be done.

In the beginning,
Genny was the one who let her love light shine
And the one who mothered the birds and the bees;
She gave meaning to the word Life.

Genny bore a paradise with every pleasure
Until the Image came and built an artificial one.
A sad Exodus followed after Genny;
She cried to think that the paradise was lost.

The righteous Rev was the last one out
At the first sound of the trumpets.
The rapture of the honeymoon was now brief
Yet the newlyweds remained in love

They joined hands and knelt before the Son.
For what God had joined together,
Man had managed to put asunder.

The Rev comes last but Genny came first.

They were married in the end to each other

And their ring was the circle called Earth.

That's the way it was meant to be

And that's the way it will be done.

"ECHOES IN MY HEAD"

Stares and sighs

whistles and wows

flooded my mind

as I heard a voice echo,

"Look but don't touch,

for it's strictly platonic."

Smiles and words

scents and touches

erased the fear as the magic of the jazz

changed the mood to romantic.

I've known a lot of women

but I've made love to more than I have known,

mostly in my dreams or theirs.

But was this a dream?

In my ear her voice soothingly whispered,

"Are you my hero or are you my lover?"

I fondly whispered back in her ear,

"Did I make your day or will I make your night?"

Neither side yielded any pat answers, only more

stares, sighs, whistles, and wows of the mind and

more scents, touches, smiles, and words...

Look but don't touch, touch, touch, touch...

for its strictly platonic, platonic, platonic, tonic...

What a comedy!

Two loves found

for all the right reasons;

So much in common,

yet so out of season.

"It's The Not Knowing"

Curiosity is a bedrock of human nature
and it's the not knowing that actually
            killed the cat.

Shaking a boxed gift at Christmas to guess
what's inside is a side effect
            of this conundrum.

Not knowing for us is akin to man's
inability to fully accept
            the prospect of his inevitable demise.

Matthew 24:36 is hard for many to fathom when it reads:
"But concerning that day and hour
no one knows,
not even the angels or heaven,
nor the Son,
            but the Father only."

When knowledge first imbued our brains,
we felt the undeniable right of all-knowing
            came with it, but it did not.

When our mouths ask, Do you love me?
Our hearts are wired to accept only Yes.
The knowing allows us to live another day
            even if the Yes was a lie.

"I'M SORRY"

Trying to unthaw frozen affections
after a heated disagreement is
often not easy.

Saying "I'm Sorry" is naturally
expected, yet almost weightless
after a while.

Although we sometimes don't see
things eye-to-eye, I feel that
we love each other very much.

Somehow, trying to unthaw frozen
affections while saying "I'm Sorry"
doesn't seem so bad when it
concerns the one that you love
very, very much.

Please forgive me, I'm sorry.

"It's Not Complicated"

I like simple because it's so easy to see
And there is never a need to be what it's not.
Simplicity is really what love is meant to be
And to be thankful for what we've actually got.
(It's not complicated)

Wanting more than you could ever need
Is gluttony at its very best.
Being more should be our personal creed
And taking less is an unselfish test.
(It's not complicated)

Respecting our neighbors and fellow citizens is a must
But respecting ourselves should always come first.
Loving others requires a mountain of trust
Loving ourselves quenches our personal thirst.
(It's not complicated)

"LOLA"

I never expected to fall in love with someone just like me,
But she is that and so much more:
Stubborn, mischievous, sexy, contrary.
Unable to resist, I am compelled to adore.

She stole my heart against my will
And playfully tied me around her fingers.
My love for her refuses to stay still
Whenever she is near, her scent always lingers.

Soon after we met, I gave her my last name
And made her the biggest part of my family.
Since she came, life is not the same,
For we are living together quite happily.

My son introduced us a few years ago.
At first, I was leery of her incredible size.
Since then, she has continued to grow
And her breed makes her a valuable prize.

I will never love another after loving her
And I prefer to remain her number one.
She has a beautiful smile and hairy fur,
A big appetite, and is loads of fun.

She accompanies me on my daily jog
And afterwards expects the biggest treat.
I never expected to have and love a grand dog
But Lola is the best dog that stands on four feet.

"Long Poem Abstract"

Illusive freedom

Chained to the past

Is like life lost in an hourglass

    Prehistoric days

    Become modern-day living

    Historic mistakes are unforgiving

Humankind forgets

More than should be remembered

Common sense has now been surrendered

    Justice depends

    On the existence of truth

    Balanced with undeniable proof

Forgiveness begins

With relinquishing the hate

Being reborn is never too late

    Earthly riches

    Are a costly solution

    Eternal wealth is an optical illusion

Marital bliss

Is desired by all

No one is ever prepared for the fall

    Flowers bloom

    Best in soil fit to grow

    Green thumb gardeners usually know

Children grow

Best when love is their manure

Parents guarantee their love will endure

     Music stirs

     The inner soul at the very least

     And it also soothes the savage beast

Old friends

Are indeed very rare

And must be treated with tender loving care

     Pets love

     Their humans unconditionally

     And will forever remain affectionately

God speaks

To mankind in mysterious ways

His Son provides us with daily rays

     Poetry flows

     Trickling through our self-defenses

     And manipulating our five senses

Love is

That which makes us wholly divine

It is entirely a heavenly design

     Abstract art

     Is that which presents possibilities

     And enhances our poetic sensibilities

"LOVE IS ELEMENTARY"

In first grade, I fell in love with Hilda,
But she probably never knew it.
My love-at-first-sight heart wanted to build a
Home, but when I tried to speak, I blew it.

In second grade, my heart belonged to Christine,
I loved her smile and her ponytail.
She was the prettiest I'd ever seen,
And I still remember her sweet smell.

Love is elementary, I came to understand.
Hilda and Christine both ignited my fuse
In my quest to become a man,
They were also the beginning of my blues.

Whenever Cupid's arrows hit my heart,
They caused my soul to bleed.
I didn't realize it from the start
That elemental love was the real seed.

I loved Cowboys and Indians before I ever met a girl,
But I never fell in love with my horse.
Loving girls created a whole new world,
And eventually it gave me my voice.

Now I know that love is elementary
And the whole world is a stage.
Falling in love is meant to be
And it can happen at any age.

"LOVE NOTES"

There is nothing more intimate

Or sexier than a handwritten note

To the one you love.

Sometimes store-bought cards

Seem too impersonal and quick.

They can't truly express

what we really feel inside.

However, a handwritten love note

Preserves the feeling and the scent

Of our original love.

A love note says it best

And is cherished forever

By the heart and soul alike.

"A Splash of Paint"

Is all that stands between us
>is a splash of paint?

I can say I love you,
>but it's obvious that you can't

The painted makeup from your face
>can easily be removed today,

but my paint cannot be removed
>so easily for being part of my DNA

When Tarzan first met Jane
>all that mattered was their primitive romance

Why must our true affections be hidden
>in plain sight without the ghost of a chance?

I'm living day-to-day just trying to get ahead
>Only trying to stay afloat in this odd world

An unfinished life is like a splash of paint
>An unfulfilled love from a beautiful girl

A renovation sometimes requires a repainting
>Being born again in the spirit is also to renew

A splash of paint is like an anointing oil
>I wish that I could paint it all over you

"My Lovely Starship"

My soft, ebony Amazon of 1976,
Who entered my life through a one-way door,
Caused the North and the South to mix,
And the earthly galaxies of love to soar.

With her blinding light to show me the way,
And her love and devotion to steer the ship,
I aligned myself with her that day,
For an endless journey instead of a trip.

I named her my Starship but she was Hernetha,
Full of passion and immortal style,
I regret the day that I lost her,
And all the days that she drove me wild.

It's hard to go back down Memory Lane,
And relive all the love that we shared,
But once and for all I need to explain,
That I was for real and that I really cared.

She was my Starship forever and a day,
But love changed its course and ours too,
I wish that there had been another way,
To let her know that my love was very true.

"I FEEL YOU"

I can understand
your pain and identify
with your circumstances
better than you think
because I've been there too
   I Feel You!

You should always
know you can
count on me
to be there for you
to listen, to help, to lean on
   I Feel You!

When you hurt, I too feel the pain
in my head
on my face
in my heart
and all over me
   I Feel You!

"GYPSY GIRL"

Gypsy men and gypsy women are known to be fancy free

When their caravan came to town, everyone was curious to see

When I first saw her, there was never any doubt

That she was the daughter of the gypsy that Curtis sang about

Deep penetrative eyes and dark hair with a curl

She could definitely be described as a beautiful gypsy girl

We were both teenagers who were too young to know

But her beauty and my curiosity were about to steal the show

I knew right away I was under her gypsy girl spell

She stared at me until my eyes blinked and then my heart fell

She danced near me with a sultry move that took my breath away

Her mother taught her well how to own the night and rule the day

My nose opened wide with a young man's fantasy

Campfire flames danced to the music with her anatomy

I couldn't take my eyes off her as she continued to twirl

It was clear I had fallen in love with a hypnotic gypsy girl

She beckoned me to run away and follow her caravan

I was only seventeen but I was determined to be her gypsy man

Seventeen-year-old Sarina lured me away with her siren touch

She pushed the limits of my heart and made it pound so much

She continued to dance to the guitar picker's melody

My mind was blown and foggy without any clarity

My journey to be a man led me to another world

And I was forever in the arms of a beautiful gypsy girl

From that day forward everyone called me a cool gypsy man

For I played the guitar that fanned the flames of my own caravan

"My Heart's Not Big Enough"

My heart's not big enough to take you back and trust you again

The last time I saw my heart,
it walked through the door in your hand when you left

Only fool's give second chances to those who murdered their dreams
before

I'm not a fool and my love's not big enough to let you
kill me again with your lies

I'd rather steer clear of you and remain by myself
until I meet someone else unlike you

Someone who is not a thief of hearts or a deceiver of the truth
You never did let the truth get in the way of a good lie

And I never stood a chance because you never told the truth

"HOPSCOTCH HEARTS"

A game usually played by children and their feet
On city sidewalks where we would all meet
White chalk marked where our feet would start
While others played with their feet, I played with my heart.

Watching her ponytail bounce as she hopped along,
My heart composed the melody of a hopscotch love song
Her beautiful face smiled as she hopped like a squirrel
She was the only girl for me in the whole wide world

One foot, two feet, we each took our turn at the game
I hopped after her but I never did ask her name
A month or two later, my crush and her parents moved away
Never again did my heart ever pound that way

Hopscotch is played by children when they are glee
Heartbreak is only played by silly fools like me.

"PUBLISHED THOUGHTS"

I once overheard someone say,
"He thinks he's all this,
and he thinks he's all that."

It always makes me laugh
when someone has me
on their mind and living
in their brain, rent free.

I never spend any time worrying
or wondering about others perception
of me.

I would rather count all
my friends than count any of my foes
because life is way too short for that.

No one can live their life
without some criticism, but petty
jealousy and constant envy
takes years away from those lives
who invest in such nonsense.

I have never felt I was any more
or less than anyone else,
and I've always tried to be
all that I can be
given my mortal limitations.

Defiant and cool, I do not
want to intimidate anyone else,
but I also choose not to be
intimidated by anyone else either.

The next time I hear someone say about me,
"You think you are this or that,"
I will say, "If you really want
to know what I think, try buying
and reading one of my books
because for years I have always
published my thoughts."

"Creative Writer"

I often write creative things to remind myself

that I am alive and living, that I am here – now!

Because some days I am not quite sure,

Not certain that this life isn't an emotional dream

gone wild after my creator created me.

Am I really real or just a figment of someone else's imagination?

Yesterday, I found a brand-new penny faced up in a puddle of water.

I picked it up, made a wish, and kept it for good luck.

Why? Am I irrational? I don't know why, I just did.

Not that I am superstitious about this life or about living,

but that I wanted to see what would happen if my wish came true.

I wonder if it ever will.

I truly believe that: *The wings of a butterfly are merely the dreams come true of an optimistic caterpillar.*

When I write, my hand births every word as if the words will be my only descendants—

The sons and daughters miraculously consummated to remind others I once lived here.

The same ones I've lovingly procreated with my own hands for posterity.

Yet, I continue to write, feeling the need to create others to validate my mortal existence.

And when I finish these living notes of life, I fold them into paper rocket ships and carefully prepare them

– my unique sons and daughters –

For a short but fantastic ride through a parental but lonely world made of paper clones.

I then sail them into the air, half-hoping that someday long after I'm gone,

Someone will find the crumpled paper orphans, read them, and realize I once lived here.

Throughout all my years of living, learning, loving and listening,

billions of words and thoughts have entered my mind and passed through

my lips with different sensations and purposes.

Numbers are not my thing but I am good with words.

Some of these words made their way to pen and paper and created a life of their own.

I don't know if these words were right, wrong, good or bad,

but I do know that they were honest, real, and creative, if not true.

Furthermore, these words painted pictures that were quite introspective

And reflected my innermost feelings exactly at the time they were created.

So, after all of this, I have concluded that:

I am a creator. I am a writer. I am a creative writer!

"PENANCE"

Why me?

Why was I born to crucify myself on paper

for all the world to read?

Why must I shed my blood, sweat, and fears

on paper for all the world to see?

I'm not sure if I were blessed or cursed when I was born –

born to be a writer.

A good friend called to tell me she cried after reading one of my poems. She said it was like I had passionately written her heart's story by rekindling a pain she had long buried.

Another person told me that a certain poem of mine made him wish he had found a love like the woman I wrote about in my verse.

Yet still, someone I never met before said he laughed so hard that he screamed after reading one of my short stories.

That kind of feedback is what writers live for and probably the reason they were born in the first place: to touch the hearts, souls, and minds of people all over the world, no matter who or where they are.

If that is my penance for being a writer, then I am glad I discovered my true calling in life so that I can serve my time well.

MY GREATEST POETRY HITS
(Reprints from Previous Books)

"READING BETWEEN THE LINES OF LOVE" (1970)

LOVER, I'VE HEARD THAT A

    (I'm only saying

PICTURE PAINTS A THOUSAND WORDS

    or painting this letter

WELL, THAT MAY BE TRUE IN

    in a realistic form of words

SOME CASES, BUT THIS PICTURE

    to simply tell you that

PAINTS ONLY THREE WORDS

    I Love You!

IT'S KIND OF HARD FOR ME

    It's not too difficult

TO SAY WHAT'S REALLY ON

    to tell you this

MY MIND, SO I'M HOPING THAT

    because I'm hiding my feelings

YOU CAN READ BETWEEN THE LINES

    between the lines of love.

THIS MAY BE A SILLY WAY TO

    Now that I've told you once

TELL YOU THAT I CARE ABOUT YOU,

    I'm going to tell you again --

BUT YOU'VE GOT TO ADMIT – IT'S A SMART WAY

    I Love You.)

BECAUSE YOU'RE MY VALENTINE EVERY DAY

"Love is Like Glass Slippers"

When Prince Charming presented

Cinderella with the glass slippers,

he symbolically placed his heart in her hands.

Fragile, rare, and crystal clear,

the glass slippers perfectly

reflected his love.

The light that sparkled so brightly through the slippers

was only matched by the light that sparkled in her eyes

when she first saw them.

For in that magical moment,

Cinderella knew the value of what

the Prince had given her.

When she eagerly slid her feet inside the slippers

and found a perfect fit, it felt like magic.

And so is it with love and friendship.

It is equally rare to find someone with whom we click.

But when we do click with someone, we find that the

friendship is both delicate and crystal clear.

And as magical as it may seem, we'll

never be the same again.

In love and in life,

when you find a shoe that fits,

simply wear it.

"Love is Like Glass Slippers 2"

Fragile, rare, and crystal clear
Oh, how I wish you were still here
You left me without a safety net
And a broken heart filled with much regret;

Do I follow you and see where it may lead
Or allow my broken heart to continue to bleed
Not sure how I manage to get you back
And put our love firmly back on track;

A broken heart and a broken shoe are alike
They both abandon the body and go on strike
Both can be repaired with the right glue
I can live without the shoe but not without you;

You are the shoe that I long to wear
I continue to search for you everywhere
I won't give up as I continue to sit
Waiting for the shoe that once did fit;

Love is like glass slippers and so is my heart
Fragile, rare, and crystal clear from the start
It easily breaks when love slips away
I won't stop crying until you're back to stay.

"CHAMELEON LOVE"

Love changes like a chameleon,
It becomes whatever it touches;
Love bloats us up like helium,
And holds us tight in its clutches.

Falling in love offers no guarantee,
Your heart serves as the thermostat;
Falling in love is usually free,
But your body becomes an acrobat.

Your mind becomes a spinning wheel,
And your life becomes a whirlwind;
It's hard to tell if love is real,
When love becomes your only friend.

A chameleon is best described as a lizard,
It charms its prey into submission;
Love was created by a wizard,
Who casts his spells without permission.

Chameleons and love are synonymous,
It's the nature of who they are;
Love and chameleons are autonomous,
It's their duty to be bizarre.

"Umbilical Cord"

Matthew 19:6

speaks of a model marriage without divorce –

a modern-day miracle to say the least.

Yesterday, Adam's rib was enough to sustain Eve

after the serpent appeared in the garden with the poison apple.

Today when the serpent appears,

all the ribs in the kitchen can't keep us from

cutting the umbilical cord – that vital lifeline

which connects Husband and Wife at the birth of a marriage.

Everyone knows a vowed marriage can only be severed by death,

but the serpent modernized and changed the shape of his

poison apples to the form of legal misnomers.

The red tasty ones are dubbed irreconcilable differences.

The delicious yellow ones are called incompatible lifestyles.

And the green tart ones are named non-commensurate educations.

They are all equally poisonous but convenient alibis to legally sever

the umbilical cord of marriage when troubles appear.

Fortunately, Matthew 19:6

does not share the same legal opinion.

It simply says,

> *"Wherefore they are no more twain, but one flesh.*
> *What therefore God hath joined together, let no man put asunder."*

"BLACK GOLD"

Like Abraham, Martin, and John
Tupac, Michael, and Prince are gone;
They too left in their prime
We mourn their deaths as a crime.

Young death is a mystery
It often comes before victory;
Their return is a fairy tale
Their legacy of good will prevail.

Whitney, Aretha, and Tina
Three queens departed the arena;
Their talent set a gold standard
In them our pride was anchored.

They all answered the call
To excel before their fall;
The world is not the same
Their fame was not to blame.

Talent, Love, and Praise
Are accolades that we raise;
We lift our glasses and toast
The ones who meant the most.

Their short stay here on Earth
Was unequal to their worth;
Yet, we thank Him for their stay
And for their souls we always pray.

"Love Lines to An Iceberg"
(A Cold Love)

Trying to unthaw frozen affection

is like licking a gigantic popsicle,

Confucius might say. What a protection!

Why must love be so cold? A mere obstacle

blocking the way to a truthful heart

and causing one to fake what is felt.

A popsicle is still cold when torn apart

and sweet when it begins to melt.

But a person who is always cold

will never melt anything except away

and probably alone; never to unfold

the mystery of those who stay

      In love rather than strive to be

      That cold part of the iceberg you can't see.

"MY SIGNIFICANT OTHER"

What's significant about us
Is that you belong to me and
I belong to you, forever.
No matter what society says,
We were meant to be.
I am yours and you are mine –
S I G N I F I C A N T L Y.

Call what we have a common law marriage, or two soulmates who are equally yoked.

We may not be legally married, but you were meant for me and I was meant for you. I knew it instantly when we first met.

The most profound thing that I've ever experienced in my life was when I first met you. When you rode your bicycle past mine, I was drawn to you like a firefly to a lantern. My world got really small and very large simultaneously.

You complete me and we can usually finish each other's sentences. My soul feels like it's known you forever although it's only been a few years.

It is impossible for anyone to tear us apart. I would rather lose my life than to lose you.

You are my safety blanket. You are my pacifier. You are my umbilical cord, my lifeline.

I cannot see me going through life without you. There is nothing or no one more important to me than you.

In my world, there is only you and me. We control our own universe and guard each other with our lives.

Until the end of our time here on earth and beyond that, I will only give myself to you.

What love has joined together, let no one else put asunder, literally.

And I do love you with no fear of our love ever fading. I significantly thank you for being my significant other.

"LIFE PARTNERS"

In Life

Everyone needs a partner –

Someone to talk to

Confide in

Walk with

Believe in

Hold onto

Someone to –

LOVE.

In this life

YOU are MY

Life Partner

People often talked about the two of them when they were together in public, but they didn't seem to care. They were life partners who were oblivious to the world around them. They lived within their own matrix which served as their whole, special world.

Unlike others who go through life unfulfilled, they were unashamed at openly displaying their affections in public, and they defied anyone else who wanted to define their relationship. They knew that going through life solo was not meant for them.

They had no limits and would not be limited by other's social mores or moral codes.

Every day they lived the meaning of ride-or-die lovers, and they knew that in death they would still prefer to be together – wherever they landed. They were unconcerned about the afterlife because they knew their love had been ordained by the universe.

A life partner is like a birth mark: a skin-deep designation that develops soon after a person is born.

In the end, it may finally prove that these life partners were in perfect harmony while everyone else was out of tune.

"Heroes And Lovers"

Heroes
are best remembered
by their incredible
     feats;
Lovers
are best remembered
by their indelible
     words.
Both are immortal.

Heroes may always
save the day;
while lovers always
come what may.

Lovers do work
to steal our
     heart;

Heroes give us
a brand-new
     start.

Lovers give love
for us to
     keep;

Heroes we dream of
when we
       sleep.

Lovers can be
from either
       gender;
Heroes can too
with names like
       Brenda.

In the end,
Heroes always
       win;
Lovers win too
when love
       begins.

"Today I Met A Girl"

Today I saw a Girl –
Young, Pure, and Impressionable.
Warmly, her smile singed my soul
as her beauty fondly made me reminisce
how it feels to be infatuated:

    It feels just like love

      so right, so genuine, so magical,

      yet, the magic often fades when the mysteries unfold.

Flowers, candy, and kisses are initially
cherished above all, but even they yield
when true love does not exist.
I suppose candid convictions are more preferred
than candied rhetoric, kindly coated with sweet, illusive truths.

Today I met a Girl –
Inexperienced, Eager, and Optimistic.
Softly, she held my hand and her touch
made me wonder what makes love real:

    If true infatuation is manufactured feelings

    manifested by fickle emotions, then

    real love must be made of that which is

    divine: blind trust, faith, and prayer.

Today I let a Girl –

Loving, Original, and Stable

enter my world through an invisible door.

Gracefully, she walked in and again,

I placed the reins in my heart's hands:

      Starting anew with a new love is never easy

      when hurt lingers freshly, but to start over

      is to love again. New faith gives way

      to new trust and old hurt becomes healed with forgiveness.

Although today I saw, met, and let

A Girl singe, touch, and enter my world,

I feel I have just discovered a new Lady.

"Hey Man, I Love You"

Yesterday, I wrote my best friend a letter

and signed it, Yours truly.

After I mailed it, I wondered why I didn't sign the

letter with love.

After all, he is my best friend and I do love him.

Then I wondered if my stubborn male pride had made

me too ashamed to tell another man I love him.

But he's not just another man, he's my best friend.

I suppose I was trying to find another way to tell him

I love him without actually saying I love him

so that my meaning could not be misconstrued.

But how can love be misconstrued?

Why didn't I just say what I feel?

We've been friends for over 25 years.

It might have been easier when we were younger,

but I never told him then either.

I may never get another chance to tell him than now.

After all, he is my best friend and I do love him.

Today, I'll write another letter and this time I'll say,

"Hey man, I love you!"

"What is Brotherly Love?"

I love my brothers in a special way
I'm not talking about the way others say
This love is true with room to grow
Unlike the quiet love only the down-low know.

Loving your brother is like loving yourself
For self-pride is required for mental wealth
To be free to love your brother is God's plan
There's nothing wrong with loving another man.

My brothers unconditionally love me back I feel
Our blood is thick and our bond is real
Others may question or even doubt
But I know what I'm talking about.

What is brotherly love you may inquire?
It's the burning inside like a warm fire
To know your brothers will always be there
Whenever you need them and they'll always care.

"The Walls That Love Built"

My treasure is now safe!

As far as the human eye can see,

An impenetrable wall encircles my well-guarded treasure–

My heart.

Is it a fort or a fortress?

It makes no difference to the attackers.

These walls were built as a defense mechanism

Against those who trespass and plunder—

Against those who leave pain instead of pleasure—

Against those who rob and leave the lights on—

Against those who … well, against everyone!

Burning these walls with fiery old flames

Yields no instant admission.

Scaling these walls with intent to do malice

Provides only a rungless ladder to descend.

Smashing these walls with sticks and stones

Reflects no visible scars on its forcefield.

Robbed once before, this treasure will never be robbed again,

And my walls guarantee that it won't.

Built by a very shrewd but foolish architect,

These walls not only keep others out,

But they also keep the treasurer hidden from other treasures.

Are they diamonds or fool's gold?

It makes no difference to these walls.

"The Wisdom of Understanding"

Sometimes,

unspoken words say more than realized

and spoken words say less than actually meant.

But when the wisdom of silence and understanding

touches lips, words disintegrate and matter very little.

Beautiful women can make men do crazy, stupid things.

A handsome man can reduce the most mature woman to become girly and giddy.

When Mother Nature is at work, no one is safe from her magic charms and spells.

Opposites attracting each other is the way nature planned it, and everyone is susceptible to falling in love.

Soft music, sweet perfume, a starry night, and a full moon are just convenient enablers to help set the mood or stage the environment, but are not required when true love is upon us.

The wisdom of understanding understands and appreciates the wisdom behind falling in love. It is an indescribable feeling that surpasses anything else on earth or beyond the universe when caught up in its rapture.

People have fallen dramatically in love with just a glance or a mere touch of a hand without uttering any words. Words are not necessary to fall in love. Only a complete understanding and acceptance of the experience that is transcending one's life into something other-worldly is required.

Being blind or deaf does not hinder one from experiencing true love.

When someone special comes, our heart opens up like a door,

and pulls the welcome mat safely on the inside.

And when someone special leaves, that same heart shrinks

to the size of a pin and sticks itself to bleed.

"L. U. S. T.
(LOVE U STILL TOMORROW)

I've loved a thousand women,
but mostly in my dreams or theirs;
the touch of your virgin lips
pushed my odometer back to zero
when we met and made our covenant

I've never known anyone like you before,
Or anything like you made me feel;
the electricity of you inside of me,
revived my heart to a level unknown
by modern medicine or sexual healing

Wherever I go I think of you,
And I feel you inside of me;
two hearts beat inside my chest
and the love I feel is protected
by the secret of you in my soul

The difference between love and lust
is something I will not reveal;
your secret is safe with me,
and your unmatched love for passion
surpasses all to become my one desire.

"Love Me Because I Love You"

Sometimes it's not enough to just love someone,

Especially when you feel love is not reciprocal.

And it's no fun loving just for fun

Unless you're expecting a miracle –

Although I can't make you love me,

Please love me because I love you.

I promise to always make you feel free

To do the things you need to do –

Loving me is not a quantum leap,

For my love is honest, real and true.

I pray for you before I sleep so

Please love me because I love you –

"SECRET SECRETS"

No one has ever known that I love you –
Not even myself.
I guess my feelings felt that I would betray
Them by telling someone else.

Because no secret keeps its secrecy
When it's told,
Even my feelings know that –
That's why they keep themselves under control.

Like a window, my feelings look at you
From both sides with much regret,
For I long to tell you I love you,
But to keep things quiet, it remains a *secret* secret.

"SCATTERED REFLECTIONS"

Scattered reflections mean more than viewing
                    thousands of pieces of broken glass;

Collectively, they represent thrown about thoughts
                    and fleeting images of past golden days.

A solid love affair can very well be
                    shattered when troubles in paradise pass;

Trying to pick up the pieces after it's broken
                    becomes a hard task to repair in many ways.

Tattered lives and *battered* emotions are often the result
                    of fragile hearts made broken;

Even the love and memories of good days gone by
                    cannot replace the heartache now felt.

Remembering that it is better to give than to receive,
                    is only an old adage that serves as a token;

For efforts in rekindling an unwilling candle are futile,
                    if they, like wax, begin to melt.

Scattered reflections never reassemble themselves after being broken.

"PERCEPTION"

Who would perceive life inside a peanut,

Or look to find freedom inside a shell?

Probably one who believes that honey is in a coconut,

Or the color of a rose does not determine its smell.

And what in him sparked HIS interest to make him see?

Possibly his belief and his humbleness,

Or maybe his genuine sincerity.

Whatever HE had perceived, he went on to confess.

The life of the peanut was soon illuminated,

But freedom was still far behind,

Yet, HIS spark of interest was communicated,

As it forever remained in his mind.

> For just as the sheep of the shepherd are spread in herds,
>
> He used the peanut (among other things) to spread HIS words.

(Written upon leaving the Dr. George Washington
Carver Museum in Tuskegee, Alabama, 1977)

"SOLO"

At times we may have to sing alone in order

To be heard above the others. It's not

The song that we sing that will make us known,

But the way that we sing it.

Not too soft and not too high.

Or not too low and not too loud.

Even though life may seem like a solo for some,

It is a song worth singing.

For who can tell,

It may finally prove that we are in perfect harmony

While everyone else is out of tune.

"PLEASE, TUNE ME BACK IN"

Lately, it seems we are on different wavelengths.

Our signals are strong, but we are going in two different directions.

Our fuzzy logic is no longer logical,

and our latitudes and longitudes have been lost.

Maybe it's just me. Am I too far out of range to receive your signals?

If so, will you adjust my antenna, wiggle my dish, play with my remote,

Or whatever it takes to tune me back in.

Please, tune me back in so that I can be on your frequency.

"Forbidden Fruit"

From afar, I admired the beautiful tree,

and I longed to get nearer for a better look.

From behind the fence, I adored the luscious fruit,

so, I climbed the fence to get even closer.

The warning signs were all around,

but I ignored them to get even nearer.

A piece of the forbidden fruit

broke loose by itself and rolled next to me.

I picked it up and held it in my hands

       p l a t o n I c a l l y.

With no intentions of eating it,

I began to crave a piece and then I took a small bite.

As I devoured the fruit, I became the fruit

and it became me – we were one.

From then on, I was ripe with desire,

and I longed to be with other forbidden fruit.

The only thing forbidden now is

my will to return to the innocence I once had.

I am the sinful, forbidden fruit,

and I will be here

       f o r e v e r.

"Free Spirits"

Broken perches, changing climates, and hungry minds
are general reasons why birds take flight.

Seeking strands of straw to build their nest or
food to feed their minds, they sometimes land near us.

Possibly birds are like us. And if they are, I'm
sure there are other things that make them soar to higher heights.

Although they don't stay long and they're not ours to keep,
it's nice to see one land in our backyard; thus,

Birds connote freedom just like children, heaven
and flags on poles.

Birds are meant to wander, to fly solo, and to
frequently change their homes.

Like them, we are often compelled by an inner
drive to reach our goals.

And when we do, yesterday becomes a pathway
to much greater domes.

"WITH NEW EYES"

When I first saw You, I didn't notice the real YOU;

I only saw a familiar face attached to a fatigued body

Like mine: worn, weary, and withdrawn.

      In You, I saw a mirror image of myself more than I saw

The face that represented You. But now, after knowing You better,

      My vision has been enhanced by Your individual beauty.

With new eyes, I see You as a humble friend who

      Unselfishly puts others before Your own special needs.

I see you as a soft candlelight that touches others

With your care and causes a chain reaction similar to

      A Domino Effect.

I can see through You, to Your soul, and know that

Your heart is pure; I can actually feel your aura as it

      Encircles Your face and permeates your body.

And I see you tomorrow as You change only to remain

      The same, realizing that love is a renewed faith in life.

With new eyes, I see You, I see Me

      Walking together, hand-in-hand, heart-to-heart,

      Looking forward to the day that we become ONE.

"SPACE"

Sometimes
I need mine
and you need yours,
I understand.

Occasional breathers
are good for any
relationship
so neither one
ever feels crowded.

However, I hope the
breathers are brief,
for I wouldn't want
anyone else to ever crowd my
S P A C E.

"FIREFLIES"

On almost quiet

crickety, summer nights

of dimly-lit skies

that resemble both solitude and despair,

tiny bursts of light *flicker* about like

flashes of new inspiration or like

ideas of hope conveniently appearing

so we can *see* that all is never lost.

Where do fireflies come from?

Where do they get their light?

I wonder if fireflies ever experience *burn-out?*

"A SOMETHING FOR NOTHING WORLD"

The human quest for an endless favor

Without offering a hand to repay the deed done,

Makes this world four-seasoned without savor.

That selfish myth deceives almost everyone,

But there are some still chivalrous,

untainted by the thought of money and material things

being obtained through means that are often hideous

and with the desire to truly earn their wings.

Still there are those who seek the light load and

Low risk street, never to give, only to receive;

but soon judgment will come and we all must stand

on our own two feet and begin to heave

> Our way into the coal yards or the vineyards as payment

> For something for nothing is only a figment.

"WEDDING DAY DUET"

On this day
We will be joined by the songs we sing
As we tune our voices for this melody.
We both sing solos for the King
But today we will sing in harmony.

Your solo is a song of Beauty
And mine a song of Love.
Together we will make a rhapsody,
And continue to sing for God above.

There will be no need for two solos,
For we will make one duet.
There will be all joy on this day
That we will never forget.

"Jumpin' The Broom"

When we first jumped the broom
My laces were untied-
I tripped over the handle
And landed on my bride-

Everyone laughed except me
They felt sorry for my wife-
Said she deserved a better sweeper
For the rest of her life-

Things got better as time went on
I became a smoother sweeper-
And when the rabbit died
I knew my wife was a keeper-

Our family now grew with a child
The one thing that made us whole-
Now when people see us
I make sure the truth is told-

When we first jumped the broom
My laces were untied-
I untied them on purpose
To land on my bride-

"Keeping A Hold On My Soul"

I don't believe in love at 1st sight
Or even at 2nd sight for that matter
I can feel love when it's right
When it's not, I select another batter.

I keep a tight rein on my soul
And rarely allow it to run free
I find I have to keep it under control
If not, I'd unleash the real me.

The world is not ready for that day
When I finally open Pandora's Box
When I truly give my heart away
I'm going to be crazy like a fox.

On the outside I appear to be cool
But inside my soul is running wild
Aching to release my inner fool
Yet the world will have to wait awhile.

"Love Sketches"

I drew a picture of my dream girl lying on a bed of roses

And then I drew her on a pedestal in several different poses;

Art imitating life is what I'm trying to pursue

That is the best way for my dream to finally come true;

My artistry lightly strokes my canvas with a brush

Bringing forth a palette of colors that is so lush;

My vision is surrounded by lush and flair

There has never been a girl like her anywhere;

What else is there for a man to draw

Than the most beautiful girl he never saw?

I won't stop until it is finally clear

That I want my dream girl standing here;

Everyone will see that I'm on a roll

When my love and I take our stroll;

Off the canvas and down by the sea

Where my love and I were meant to be;

Life imitating art is the final act

The picture of love is complete and intact.

"CANVAS LADY"

On canvas,

I painted the most beautiful girl that never lived.

With every orgasmic stroke of seminal paint,

I made her come

Alive before my eyes.

I always dreamed of having a girl like her.

The more I painted, the more she came,

Alive!

Naked, she fell from the canvas and became real.

I painted on some jeans and a sexy silk blouse to go with her bare feet.

We walked away hand-in-hand on our way to the beach.

A needle in a haystack is hard to find; soulmates are even harder.

She had a beautiful face, but an even more beautiful soul.

I will forever cherish this pot of gold.

"Who Knew Then?"

Walked through the park where we first met
Our names still etched in our favorite tree;
That was long ago before my regret
Who knew then who we would be?

You grew into a famous beauty
And I became a famous writer;
Together we were very snooty
But our future was never brighter;

We got married and built a castle
Not far from where we once played;
Our lives became a hassle
And our storybook love began to fade;

Who knew then how we would end?
And live our lives separately;
The park is gone and with it went
Our favorite tree and our revelry.

"Remembering Eden"

From six degrees of separation

To two degrees of admiration,

Our untrained hearts

Strayed into a Garden of Eden;

With hearts untrained to lie and

Hide what they felt, we discovered

The naked truth about what lies beneath the taboo.

In the darkness, we tasted the nectar

Of the fruit we bore and was mesmerized

By the words, perfume and proximity;

Nothing else mattered and time stood still for a second.

With one body and two hearts we felt the rapture

Of the moment and realized the urgency and the power

Within our grasp -- A final kiss, a lasting embrace and

A lifetime love gave birth to a special bond.

That night young hearts ran free as wiser minds

Pledged to retain the love and respect without

Compromising what was born out of freedom.

May we never forget the night we were joined as One.

"LOVE ON MARS"

My love feels like I'm beyond the stars
Reaching to higher heights with every kiss—
Any higher and I'll be loving on Mars
And this old Earth I'll never miss;
My body feels like I'm in a dream
And I'm floating weightlessly—
The gaze in my eyes is like a beam
And I'm headed toward my destiny;
Nothing on Earth ever made me swoon
My breath was never taken away—
I am somewhere beyond the moon
And believe me I want to stay;
If love on Mars is my secret place
I plan to live there forevermore—
I hope they never find a single trace
Of me, my love and our secret door;
I'm saying goodbye to you my friend
And never coming back to Earth—
This feeling is real and not a pretend
I have experienced a brand-new birth.

"GOD INSIDE ME"

Ever since I was young, I've felt a specialness in my soul

This feeling flowed through me like a quiet fire out of control;

Someone watched over me and held me in high esteem

I felt highly favored and a valued member of His team;

As I got older, I felt my heart stray away

And lose the closeness that I used to feel every day;

But at night in my dreams, I heard His voice

Reminding me that I was still his favorite choice;

I didn't feel I really deserved His mercy and grace

But He said that I would always have a place;

It was God's eyes on me and God inside me

That led to His kingdom and my natural destiny;

I could no longer escape what He had in store

So, I accepted my fate and longed to be more;

I now know that divine intervention is not a myth

In His image I was made to always be with;

Upon acceptance of His parental love and holy touch

I gained abundance in my life and never needed much;

There's no end to this experience that I am telling

For in my Father's house, I will forever be dwelling.

"In Reverence"

In memory of a well-lived life
Whose soul is now free from strife;
May God have mercy on his soul
And let him walk the streets of gold;
Nearer to God now is he
What a wonderful place to be;
Precious Lord please take his hand
Allow his memory to always stand;
We pray that his soul will rest in peace
And our undying love will never cease;
He now walks among God's chosen few
And lives in a place that is divinely new;
We sing this song for his home going
With God's speed there is no slowing;
Ashes to ashes and dust to dust
In God we pray and in God we trust.

"THERE IS NO FINISH LINE"

Before a race is run, we usually mark off our course and set the time,
But in life we learn there are no such parameters and no such endline.

Finish lines enable false starts and pipe dreams of coming in first;
However, the race is about having the stamina to run past the thirst.

Stopping at a specific distance is the normal measure of a race well run,
But in life stopping does not signify the end of the race because it is never done.

When we sit on our laurels and showcase our trophies, we don't act like winners.
In life, the real trophies go to those who always see themselves as beginners.

We should condition ourselves to run past any preset endline set for us.
We should know that coming in dead last should be viewed as a plus.

Knowing that the last shall be first is the understanding of a virtue.
The virtue of coming in last is the symbol of our victory statue.

There is no finish line because life is a cycle without a real finish
Even after our lives on Earth are through our spirits do not diminish.

So, get rid of any notion that a finish line signifies you are through.
Keep on running to the best of your ability until life begins anew.

ABOUT THE AUTHOR

sketch by Eddye K. Allen,
Expressions of Eddye K.
allen.keddye@gmail.com

Alabama-born American author JAMES L. THOMPSON, JR. describes himself as an "extroverted-introvert." He's been writing since 1970 when he penned his first poem in a 10th grade English class that was published in the school paper. He enjoys writing and playing with words and wordsmithing is part of his unique writing style. Although he has distinguished himself in many separate careers, he was born to be a writer because that is his passion.

This is Thompson's 5th book and he is in rare form with poetry being his first love and his mistress. Thompson's unique voice is a welcomed addition among the many voices that write poetry and tell lyrical stories. His new book publishing company, Peanut City Press, LLC, is a perfect book outlet for talented creative voices like his and other up and coming talent. Let Peanut City Press be the cradle of your creativity.

ACKNOWLEDGMENTS

With my 5th book and new all-poetry book (2025), I worked with a collaborative, international team of extraordinary talent. Phenomenal canvas artist Justin from Philadelphia custom-painted the shack on my front book cover, master photographer Kevin from Newtown photographed me for the back cover, extraordinary book cover artists from Ukraine designed my book cover, multi-talented Katherine from Nigeria formatted my book, professional and generous sketch artists Dumith from Sri Lanka and Hizachi from Algeria drew the great art sketches for my book, Black Wall Street artist Eddye K from Tulsa drew a sketch of me for my author's page, supreme video editor Roziqin from Indonesia created my video book trailer, my longtime friend, Mit Kirkland from Dothan allowed me to use his song, "Forever More" for my video book trailer, and my creative director son, Jaye, from Brooklyn created my website. I feel that my 50 plus years of writing poems climaxed with this new deluxe imprint and I am proud to share our collective talents with the world. Thank you for all the support that you have given me and Peanut City Press, LLC.

www.ingramcontent.com/pod-product-compliance
Lightning Source LLC
Chambersburg PA
CBHW020854090426
42736CB00008B/366